X

NOTES AND ESSAYS ON EDUCATION FOR ADULTS **70**

RESIDENTIAL CONTINUING EDUCATION

CYRIL O. HOULE

Syracuse University
PUBLICATIONS IN CONTINUING EDUCATION

A Publication in Continuing Education
Syracuse University

MELVIN A. EGGERS, *Chancellor*

ALEXANDER N. CHARTERS, *Vice President for Continuing Education*

DORIS S. CHERTOW, *Editor, Publications in Continuing Education*

RESIDENTIAL CONTINUING EDUCATION

DISCARD

by
CYRIL O. HOULE
Professor of Education
The University of Chicago

September 1971

Syracuse University
PUBLICATIONS IN CONTINUING EDUCATION

For information about publications in continuing education published by
Syracuse University and the Center for the Study of Liberal Education
for Adults, write to the Editor, Syracuse University Publications in
Continuing Education, 105 Roney Lane, Syracuse, New York 13210.
Syracuse University distributes CSLEA publications.

LIBRARY OF CONGRESS CATALOGUE CARD: 71-171883

Copyright 1971

Syracuse University Publications
in Continuing Education

Additional copies of this book may be ordered from:
SYRACUSE UNIVERSITY PRESS
Box 8, University Station
Syracuse, New York 13210

ISBN: 0-87060-045-1   Price: $ 3.00

TO

MAURICE F. SEAY

a continuing pioneer of continuing education

The general principles of any study you may learn by books at home; but the detail, the colour, the tone, the air, the life which makes it live in us, you must catch all these from those in whom it lives already . . . As regards the world of science, we find a remarkable instance of [this principle] in the periodical meetings . . . such as [those of] the British Association. Such gatherings would to many persons appear at first sight simply preposterous. Above all subjects of study, Science is conveyed, is propagated, by books, or by private teaching; experiments and investigations are conducted in silence; discoveries are made in solitude . . . Yet . . .not even scientific thought can dispense with the suggestions, the instruction, the stimulus, the sympathy, the intercourse with mankind on a large scale, which such meetings secure. A fine time of year is chosen, when days are long, skies are bright, the earth smiles, and all nature rejoices; a city or town is taken by turns, of ancient name or modern opulence, where buildings are spacious and hospitality hearty. The novelty of place and circumstance, the excitement of strange, or the refreshment of well-known faces, the majesty of rank or of genius, the amiable charities of men pleased both with themselves and with each other; the elevated spirits, the circulation of thought, the curiosity; the morning sections, the outdoor exercise, the well-furnished, well-earned board, the not ungraceful hilarity, the evening circle; the brilliant lecture, the discussions or collisions or guesses of great men one with another, the narratives of scientific processes, of hopes, disappointments, conflicts, and successes, the splendid eulogistic orations; these and the like constituents of the annual celebration, are considered to do something real and substantial for the advance of knowledge which can be done in no other way . . . They issue in the promotion of a certain living and, as it were, bodily communication of knowledge from one to another, of a general interchange of ideas, a comparison and adjustment of science with science, of an enlargement of mind, intellectual and social, of an ardent love of the particular study, which may be chosen by each individual, and a noble devotion to its interests.

Cardinal John Henry Newman

John Henry Newman, University Sketches (Dublin: Browne and Nolan, Ltd., undated, text of 1856), pp. 9-12.

The   theme of this discursive essay is residential continuing education:
its definition; its development along somewhat different lines in Europe and in
America, and its practice in university centers in the United States. The
most significant influence in the growth of such centers has been the sustained
interest of the W. K. Kellogg Foundation; and this issue of Notes and Essays
is a by-product of a project supported by that Foundation at the University
of Chicago.

The Studies and Training Program in Continuing Education was directed
briefly by George W. Aker (now of Florida State University) and, for most
of its tenure, by Ann Litchfield (now of Oregon State University). Its aim
was to foster the growth of university activities in residential continuing
education and it sought to achieve this purpose in many ways, chiefly by:
providing internships in The University of Chicago Center for Continuing
Education; influencing graduate students in adult education and other fields;
conducting studies; issuing reports; organizing conferences; and working with
national associations. The sponsors of this Program hope that it has had
substantial influence in helping to shape the thought of modern university-
based residential continuing education.

During my association with the Program throughout its fourteen years of
existence, I had ample opportunity to reflect about the significance of this
method of learning in adulthood and therefore eagerly seized the opportunity
offered when the editor of Notes and Essays asked me to write this paper.
Most of the illustrations are drawn from the Chicago experience, and my
reliance on the work of many people, both here and elsewhere, is evident in
the essay itself. As always, my wife provided help and support throughout.
Dolores Ford typed many versions of all or part of the document with her
usual competence and helpfulness. Beatrice Raynor typed the final version
for Publications in Continuing Education. The following people criticized a
first draft: Harold J. Alford, Thomas P. Bergin, John H. Buskey, Doris

S. Chertow, Ann Fales, Lucy Ann Geiselman, William S. Griffith, Ann Litchfield, Philip Nowlen, Dorothy Sickels, and Thurman J. White. Countless others who must go unnamed have helped to shape the ideas it expresses. I am grateful to all of them, but the responsibility for the essay is wholly my own.

The greatest debt, which all of us in the field owe collectively, is to the board and staff of the W.K. Kellogg Foundation who, for a quarter century, have demonstrated their belief in residential continuing education.

Cyril O. Houle
Professor of Education
The University of Chicago

TABLE OF CONTENTS

I. DEFINITIONS AND DISTINCTIONS

Short-term integrated continuing residential education for groups, the actual subject of this essay, might be called, in these days of acronyms, STICREG. Despite its brevity and mnemonic function, however, the term is ugly and its use pretentious. Therefore, "residential continuing education" or "residential education" will be used as symbols for the longer and more precise term, but a clarification of what it means will help to define the framework of this essay.

Continuing education includes any learning or teaching program which is based on the assumptions that the learners have studied some related body of content previously and that they wish to carry on the process further. Since most such people are adults, "continuing education" is sometimes used as a synonym for "adult education," but the latter term has a broader, more flexible meaning than the former, including as it does all those individual, group, and institutional ways by which men and women seek to learn or teach.

Since adults are normally engaged in meeting the complex demands imposed upon them by home, work, and community, their learning must accompany these primary activities or be fitted in among them. Sometimes this fitting-in is an interruption; the adult leaves home to live for a while in a learning environment wholly different from that which customarily defines his life pattern. Practical considerations usually make it necessary for him to spend only a short time away from his normal environment. Thus, while residential education can stretch out to a period of years or even to a lifetime of monastic study, it customarily has a compass of from one day to several months.

The degree to which educational activities are intentionally integrated with normal processes of living to create a total learning environment varies greatly. Four patterns are common. One group may live and study in a center so structured that all the normal socially-sanctioned processes of daily life are designed to advance or aid learning. A second group may live

1

in a facility not directly part of the study center but closely enough   related
to it so that the intellectual and social relationships reinforce one another.
A third group may live together in a hotel and go to an educational institution
for meetings, but have no other intellectual activities in common and share
only a minimal social life. A fourth group may be made up of individuals who
live wherever they independently choose and go to the institution only for
scheduled sessions. While all four; groups of learners, living away from
home and taking part in an institution-centered program, can be considered
to be engaged in residential education, this essay will concentrate chiefly
on the first and second of the four since they offer the most complete kind
of integrated life-and-learning situations.

While some residential learning is almost completely individualized, as
in some of the centers for advanced study, it is so preponderantly intended
for groups that only this latter form will be considered here.

Residential education is one of the four patterns an individual most
commonly uses when he seeks to learn, the other three being self-instruction,
tutorial study, and course-taking. In all four, the educative process follows
a common series of steps which moves analytically, though not always
temporally, from the selection of goals to the appraisal of what has been
accomplished, but each pattern has its distinctive nature and is characterized
by a unique set of values.

Sometimes a pattern is imposed by the situation, but at other times it
is chosen. For example, when people from widely separated geographic
areas are to be brought together, a conference may be the only possible form
of education. In other cases residential learning may be selected in pre-
ference to another pattern because of particular values claimed for it.
Some of them are: it provides an intensive and concentrated experience;
it makes possible the use of scarce human and material resources; it takes
people away from their routines and enlarges their horizons; and it gives
them the opportunity to make valuable continuing associations outside their
home communities. Other less immediately evident values will be mentioned
in later pages.

It can also be argued that residential continuing education has inherent

2

disadvantages when compared with one of the other patterns of learning. For
example, in contrast to a course which a learner may take in his home
community, it is sometimes said that: the residential conference is more
expensive; it requires a greater readjustment of the life-pattern of the participants; it cannot reach as many people; it is not a good way to master physical
skills such as typing or piano playing; it concentrates learning rather than
spacing it out for better absorption; it deprives the student of the continuing
interaction between theory and practical affairs; it limits the variety of
teaching resources and techniques; and it tends to encapsulate learning as an
activity removed from the flow of life and not really affecting it. Such inherent
drawbacks, it is argued, may not be universal, but they are so pervasive
that they can be surmounted, if at all, only by inspired leadership.

Efforts to compare patterns may be useful in helping to refine distinctions
among them, but to pit them against one another assumes that one of them is
inherently best and should ultimately prevail over the others. It is more useful to consider them all as parts of a broad educational design. In times
past, the scarcity of resources meant that institutions and people had to
concentrate on a single method of study. Now, with the continuing enrichment
of opportunities in the expanding economy of adult education, the attitude is
changing. More and more institutions include residential education as one
element of their work. More and more individuals accept periodic conference
attendance as an integral part of their continuing education. And in the
development of long-range educational opportunities (such as the shaping of
career lines in the professions, the provision of special external baccalaureate
or master's degrees, or the training of management personnel in industry)
it is expected that use will be made of all four patterns of learning in many
of the variations and adaptations of design appropriate to each.

II.   THE EUROPEAN EXPERIENCE

The idea of residential continuing education has been discovered afresh
in many times and places. The world's literature contains countless reports
of the rise of programs or institutions, each standing alone, its creators
often unaware that it had parallels. But the eye of the historian discerns
one clear line of sequential development beginning in Denmark in the middle
of the ninet eenth century and deepening and spreading its influence ever
since until now it is a world-wide movement, differing in important ways in
each setting and each country in which it is found and yet having a fundamental unity of thought and practice.[1]

The roots of this lengthening tradition were European and humanistic,
but as the idea of residential continuing education has been transplanted from
one culture to another, it has taken on a unique pattern and coloring in each
new setting in which it survived. This change occurred in the first such
movement, when the Danish folk high school was imitated across the Öresund
in Sweden, where, as W.R. Fraser notes , "There was less emphasis on
patriotism and godliness and song, and more attention to good general
knowledge, science, objectivity and to diplomas or courses that advance
students in such careers as nursing, police, civil service, welfare work. "[2]
This essay cannot deal with the world-wide permutations of the idea, but will
present only an interpretation of the original concepts developed in Denmark,
their generalization into a broad European tradition, and the marked changes
which occurred when the tradition became established in American culture.

Many theorists have written about the meaning of residential education,
but the works of two have achieved pre-eminence. One was N.S.F. Grundtvig,

---

[1] The major comprehensive history of this world-wide movement is:
Harold J. Alford, "A History of Residential Adult Education" (unpublished
doctoral dissertation, The University of Chicago, 1966).

[2] W.R. Fraser, Residential Education (Oxford: Pergamon Press, 1968),
p. 206.

a stormy young pastor working near (and sometimes beyond) the boundaries
of tolerance of nineteenth century national and religious life in Denmark. The
other was Richard Livingstone, a classical scholar, a knight, the administrative head of an Oxford college and then of Oxford itself, and, by the time of
his leadership in residential continuing education, a man of almost unearthly
remoteness and quietness of temperament. Neither man was involved in the
administration of residential continuing education, and may never have even
participated in it except as a lecturer, observer, or ceremonial figure, but
each spoke in a way which could be understood and acted upon at a crucial
time in his country's life. Perhaps (particularly in Sir Richard's case) the
ideas expressed were already evident in many other men's minds and actions,[1]
but they were put so clearly and effectively by the two major spokesmen
that they had an immediate impact and have been remembered ever since.

Bishop Nicolaj F.S. Grundtvig

For the Danes, the first two-thirds of the nineteenth century was a time
of constant struggle and recurrent catastrophe. The country became involved against its will in the Napoleonic wars, during which its fleet was
seized and Copenhagen bombed. In 1813, the government went bankrupt and
in 1814 it was forced to yield   Norway, its ancient possession, to Sweden.
The Congress of Vienna in 1815 tried to resolve the complex questions of
Schleswig and Holstein, but without success. After fifty years of constant
strife over the issue, the war of 1864 cost Denmark both provinces, which
included more than a third of its territory and two-fifths of its people. Mean-
while, internal political dissension churned as an absolute monarchy was
supplanted by a constitutional regime, and economic difficulty persisted as the
peasants who had been freed from serfdom in 1788 tried to establish themselves as independent land-holders in an essentially agricultural country.

---

[1] The case for this point, so far as Sir Richard is concerned, is force-
fully put in: Donald Garside, "Short-Term Residential Colleges: Their
Origins and Value," Studies in Adult Education, I (April, 1969), pp. 10-12.

5

Throughout the whole period, recurrent crises and continuing strains gave rise to a sense of national despair.

The young Grundtvig reacted strongly against this prevailing mood. In a lifetime of writing, he expressed his ideas on many subjects, doing so in a passionate fulminating language which often seems, at least to a non-Scandinavian, to be characterized by cloudy rhetoric and mysticism. Although intensely nationalistic and filled with devotion to his king, he hated the depths of poverty, political subjugation, and defeatism to which his country had fallen. So far as education was concerned, he looked with horror at the traditional apparatus of scholarship, "the enormous book heaps which have stacked up during the last three centuries."[1] As it turned out, Grundtvig stacked up an enormous heap of his own. In its unsystematized mass, his major structural ideas are hard to discern – but it is possible to identify the conceptions which moved his followers to build institutions of residential continuing education. We see him through them.

It is crucial to an understanding of Grundtvig's thought to realize that he was not essentially concerned with residential learning as a process. He visited Oxford and Cambridge and admired their communal life, but what really impressed him was not the form but the product, the liberating effect of the education itself. The mere process of living together could not bring about the maturity of viewpoint which arose from close communion between tutor and student. Monasteries, for example, could be formal and stultifying places. Deeper, more profound ideas must be at work in the English colleges. What were they? More important, how could they be made to have a lifelong application?

He found many answers. The chief goal of education must lie beyond the mere mastery of knowledge, proceeding to the improvement of life itself. As

---

[1] This question and others from Grundtvig are taken (as is much of this analysis of his writings) from The School for Life, a collection of Nicolaj F.S. Grundtvig's key writings, published as Continuing Education Report Number Five, The University of Chicago, 1965. These reports were issued by the Studies and Training Program in Continuing Education at The University of Chicago.

people differ greatly from one another, so should the advanced specifics of their education. "A fundamentally homogeneous education," however, ought to constitute the root, producing a sense of community for all people, no matter what separate careers they may have later. Bankers, physicians, merchants, farmers, and peasants should be self-respecting persons who communicate with one another on the basis of common knowledge. Grundtvig desired that this shared foundation of learning be offered at the least expense possible, enabling everyone to participate. The Spartan nature of the physical facilities advocated for instruction would lead to a greater value being placed upon the mind and spirit. But the education must always be voluntary--and here Grundtvig is caught by one of the eternal dilemmas of humanistic education, for he argues that while each man should freely choose what he wants to learn, all men should choose the same thing.

The method of teaching, Grundtvig thought, should be the communication of ideas through powerfully expressed lectures and vivid discussions. Only when learning is embodied in people can there be a "living word" which informs and illuminates. "All letters are dead even if they are written with angelic fingers and star pens; all possible knowledge is dead where it does not fuse with an analogous life of the reader." Fraser sums up this body of thought by saying:

> For Grundtvig, the way of living as a Christian lay through a
> full life as a human being. By teaching the people through the
> language of colloquial speech and of their literary heritage
> he hoped to speak the language of the heart and so to educate their
> feelings that the rising Danish democracy, for which he believed
> God had a purpose, would avoid the excesses and chaos of
> the French Revolution and would demonstrate enlightened
> liberal democracy to the world. [1]

However grandiose this aim may have seemed when first enunciated, it was eventually achieved. The process was slow, as Grundtvig had prophesied it would be: "Of course, one may certainly doubt how far a school devoted to culture would be attended in the beginning, but the fact that one expects little or nothing of it at the outset will just contribute to its future blossoming."

---

[1]Fraser, Residential Education, p. 205.

Some of Grundtvig's ideas may have been adopted in established schools, but the first institution wholly devoted to them was created by Kristen Kold in 1851 when he founded a folk high school at Ryslinge. The students in this school and in its imitators were in their late teens and early twenties, but they had experienced five to eight years of adult responsibility after leaving their earlier schooling. Since most of them were agricultural workers, they were freed by the rigors of the Danish climate for a long period of study in winter, but were so scattered about the countryside that no one community could support a school. It had to be residential to exist, and, because of the abject poverty of its leaders and students, they had to be idealistic to survive conditions of almost unbelievable austerity. The scarcity of educational resources meant that there could be no word other than the living word.

Thus was created the embodiment of Grundtvig's ideals. Success did not come at once, but the times were so desparate that almost any innovation was examined with interest, though not necessarily with approval. Gradually the idea grew as Grundtvig had said it would: "The longer the school operates, the more and better helpers it will get around the country, and such an education will also succeed more or less everywhere we diligently nurse it. Concerning the benefits, it is with every institution as with every tree one plants that only time can show the fruits of it, and that luck is needed for everything which is to succeed and thrive." With its success, the stormy pastor became the revered bishop, and eventually one of his country's folk heroes.

For he helped prepare the way for the cultural revolution which was to transform Denmark into a model for the world. The folk high school was not the only begetter of the extraordinary changes which occurred, but even those modern Danes who most passionately deny its historical importance or present relevance to the national life cannot fail to note its power as a creative force. Temperance, better agriculture, cooperative economic systems of production and consumption, city planning, and countless other special crusades developed their own goals, institutions, and momentum. But the folk high school from its beginning dealt centrally with the total improvement of the Danes as men and women and of Denmark as a country, and thus helped provide the keystone on which the structure of a new national life could be built.

Danes carried the idea of the folk high school with them wherever they went - and for more than a thousand years they have been famous as travelers. Residential education on the Danish model spread - first through Scandinavia, then through the rest of Europe, on to the Western Hemisphere, and finally to all the world, including the newly emerging nations. Some of the most recently established adult educational institutions in Africa, for example, were founded, directed, and supported by Danes. The tradition was also reinforced by people from other lands who traveled to Denmark to observe the social transformation occurring there and often took home with them the idea of the folk high school and the determination to re-create it in their own countries.

Sir Richard Livingstone

One such visitor was Sir Richard Livingstone, who went from Oxford to Denmark in the late 1930's, thereby reversing the pattern followed more than a century before by Grundtvig. Sir Richard was greatly impressed by the folk high schools. While his study was far from thorough and exact, the important element in his observation was not what he saw in them but what he took to them: a keen and analytical mind used to abstractions and distinctions; an impatience with the established traditions of English education of which he himself was a leading exemplar; and the mastery of a clear and sinewy prose created by a lifetime of classical studies. His mind was too subtle and complex to permit him to believe in the simple translation of an institution from one culture to another and he was too steeped in his national traditions to believe that his own country would accept so unEnglish an organization as the folk high school. But some impulse or plan led him to visit Scandinavia to search for principles which could be translated into practice back home. England might boast of its world-famous schools and universities, but the general level of instruction, he thought, was deplorably

9

low. "Why are we an uneducated nation," he asked, "and how can we become an educated one?" (p. 1)[1]

The answer to this question, he believed, lay in certain ideas exemplified in the Danish system and, more particularly, in its "three secrets of success: it is given to adults; it is residential; it is essentially a spiritual force." (p. 47) While all three were equally important, Sir Richard tended to emphasize the first. He thought he perceived an ignored educational principle: "Almost any subject is studied with much more interest and intelligence by those who know something of its subject-matter than by those who do not: and, conversely, . . . it is not profitable to study theory without some practical experience of the facts to which it relates." (p. 7; italics in original) This principle explains, he said, why adults can learn in three to five months what it takes young people three to five years to master. To education, adults "bring something which no schoolboy can ever have – a fully grown intelligence, a sense of the value and meaning of education, and that practical experience of life, without which history, literature, and philosophy are lifeless phantoms." (p. 49)

The residential life of the folk high school means that the learner can live "for three to five months wholly steeped in the atmosphere of education: the dye sinks deeper and takes a more lasting hold." (p. 50) The teacher can come to know his students as individuals and work with each of them in a deeply personal sense. The community life means that "the pupils learn from each other's views and personalities, from contiguity and personal talk. . . No doubt the lamp of wisdom can burn in solitary shrines and even in dismal lecture halls. But for the many it will not burn brightly, if at all, unless fanned by that social, corporate life which exists in a residential university and which both educates and makes education attractive." (pp. 51-52) Such an education might take many forms in many places but

---

[1] All quotations are taken from Richard Livingstone, The Future in Education, which was reprinted in the United States in a single volume with another of his works under the title On Education (New York: The Macmillan Company, 1945). The location of each quotation is indicated in parentheses after it.

to the Danes it is primarily a moral spiritual force, elevating the
mind and strengthening the will by the vision of great ideals. The
two aims can never be dissociated; education, however intellectual, must always in some degree affect the outlook and through
it character and conduct . . . This idealism has its practical
uses. In the second half of the nineteenth century Denmark, with
no economic advantages, passed from depression to prosperity
and became a pioneer and model of agricultural methods . . .
The regeneration of a people is worth study, and this instance
is of special interest to educationists, for it is generally agreed
that the People's High School was one of the chief instruments
in the economic progress of Denmark. And yet the schools
seemed useless for such a purpose; they were in no sense agricultural colleges; they gave no vocational courses and their
backbone was the study of history and literature . . . They did not
teach their pupils how to farm well but they produced in them a
passionate desire to do it. Their aim was not to impart knowledge
but to awaken intelligence and idealism . . . 'When they come to
us, they are sleeping,' said the Principal of a High School to the
writer: 'it is no use teaching them while they are asleep. We
try to go to the centre, to arouse the spirit - the rest will follow.'
(pp. 53-56)

Sir Richard was no more of an institution builder than Grundtvig had

been; he drew no organizational charts and designed no building plans.

But he did specify the basic principles of a new educational system for

Britain using the Danish "secrets." It would be for adults - and for all adults

at all ages, not merely the young adults on whom the folk high schools con-

centrated. Everybody, poor or rich, needed to learn and to do so all his

life. Education would be residential, necessitating interruption of the normal

course of work and family life by periodic leaves for "systematic study in

order to refresh and re-equip and reorientate his mind." (p. 93) The

rhythm of the seasons in agricultural Denmark meant that the winter months

were available for study, but special arrangements sanctioned by a wide-

spread social committment to the idea of study would have to be found in

industrialized Britain to give men the periodic freedom to learn. For

"every moment the crust of routine is forming over the mind, thickening,

and impairing its fertility; only a continually renewed activity of thought

can break it up." (p. 101) And the education provided must be, in a broad

sense, spiritual, though not in the transcendental Danish sense. In England,
the central theme should be the development of the whole man in body,
mind, and character. Sir Richard went on to define what he meant by liberal
education in what may be the clearest, most sweeping definition of that term
provided by the literature of education. (pp. 69-70)

The little book in which these ideas were expressed, The Future in
Education, was published in 1941 in an England which seemed almost ideally
ready to receive its message. The war had then gone on for two years, but
still there was no firm basis for hope that it could ever be won. The Nazi
occupation of Europe, the rout at Dunkirk, the battle of Britain, and the
death and destruction of many of England's men and institutions had created a
national mood of depair and frustration, tempered only by a blind and dogged
courage and, quixotically, by a determination to try to plan for a better
post-war world. Much of this discussion centered on education, and the
clear, reasonable, idealistic voice of Sir Richard was powerfully influential
in winning assent for the ideas he put forward, ideas which began to spread
across the land achieving an independent life of their own and reaching many
people who may never have known their source. The People's Residential
Education Association, designed to advance such ideas, was founded in
1944 and had some effect, particularly among people having an association
with Oxford. It was a group, however, whose idealism was created by war-
time conditions and whose members were gifted with organizational skills.
It had only a single year of life and was a casualty of the   strains attendant
upon the ending of the European war [1]   but, as it turned out, the goals of
the Association were achieved with astonishing rapidity.

For, as the war drew to a close and the period of reconstruction began,
the idea of creating residential centers for short courses, from two days to
several weeks in length, seemed to arise spontaneously throughout the
country. The Education Act of 1944 had laid a mandate upon local educational

_____

[1]Laurence Speak, "Residential Adult Education in England " (unpublished
master's thesis, Leeds University, 1949), Vol. I, pp. 90-96.

12

authorities to provide liberal adult education and had given them resources to do so. (In Britain, those authorities do not merely administer education, but also make many grants to other bodies and individuals, acting in some respects like philanthropic foundations.) Many of the great old country houses had been taken over from their owners for war purposes and now became available for use; thus capital costs could be kept to a minimum. Not least in importance was the assertion of vigorous new leadership. Many of the men and women in the armed forces who had participated in adult education, some of it in residential centers, wanted to make their careers in the field. As one of them wryly observed, the great estates came on the market at the same time as the madmen whom it took to run them. These men and women, returning to the various sectors of a society which was rebuilding itself, actively supported the idea of residential continuing education centers under many auspices, among them local educational authorities, universities, voluntary associations, religious groups, and political parties. The P. R. E. A. had hoped in 1945 to establish one center; five years later, at least thirty were in existence and others were being proposed or created.

Essentials of the European Conception

This hasty history has dealt with the values of residential adult education chiefly as they were expressed in the words of two principal theorists of the movement. Now it is time to look more directly at the essential ideas of the European conception as they have evolved through practice and through a voluminuous literature. The general attributes of that conception, which are suggested below, do not take account of the great variation from one center to another, nor of the distinctive pattern developed in each country. Furthermore, each of these attributes is denied by practice in some institutions, or is refuted by an authority of experience or eminence. On balance, however, the elements listed below seem to reflect the main ideas shaped through more than a century of thought and practice.

Residential adult education requires its own physical facilities, preferably those which are devoted solely to the purpose. While courses and conferences may be held in borrowed or rented accommodations, such as the colleges of Oxford or resort hotels anywhere in Europe, the educational experience provided in such places is usually only a pale approximation of what it might be in a separate center whose traditions and practices are totally consigned to the residential education of adults.

European centers have myriad forms of sponsorship. Some are wholly independent, some are administered by traditional educational institutions, and some are operated by various branches of government, but most of them fall under the control of private or semi-public organizations and associations. As a result, residential continuing education finds its home in many parts of a country's political, economic, and social life. A sharp distinction between public and private institutions is not ordinarily found in Europe; in particular the church may be part of the government. Many residential centers therefore derive their financial support from several sources; thus, an essentially private institution addressing itself to the advancement of the working class or of fundamentalist religion may receive grants from both national and local governments.

Each center has a strong central purpose which pervades the institution and which it promotes with a sense of mission. This purpose may be highly specific, as is the case in centers concerned with socialism, conservatism, the Christian ethic, gymnastics, artistic reform, the cooperative movement, or the education of leaders for voluntary associations. The purpose may also be a general one, dealing, for example, with the provision of liberal and cultural experiences. But the aim is clear and is pervasive. When a European center must accept (usually for economic reasons) a conference not centrally related to this aim, the staff members often try to make it the focus of at least part of the program. This sense of mission helps greatly in the administration of the center. The staff members are chosen because they believe in the goal, and the sense of a common purpose helps to reduce or to solve problems of acceptance of authority, personality conflict, and

14

assignment of responsibility.

Whatever the specific sense of mission, it has a strongly humanistic quality. Learning is its own reward; formal degrees or certificates are meaningless. While rationalistic goals may be required to guide structure and content, the overriding purpose has to do with the self-discovery of the individual. From the time of Grundtvig to the present day, terms such as "awakening", "rebirth," "inspiration," "a new perspective on life," and "the education of the whole person" have been used. But while a social purpose is almost always expressed, its achievement is never sought in a mechanistic fashion. Thus, Elizabeth Brinkman of Germany said that the goal should be to help the students

> to enlarge their knowledge in individual fields of intellectual
> and practical life, to clarify and deepen it in order to provide
> 'Lebenshilfe' for a better solution of the problems of daily
> life - and to give 'help for life' in a deeper sense; i. e., to
> lead the individual out of isolation and thus to a sense of
> responsibility towards the community. [1]

As this kind of purpose is difficult to achieve in vocational courses, most European-oriented centers try to avoid sponsoring them. While some centers are wholly or partially occupational in purpose, they are thought to be different in character from the humanistic centers and are held at arm's length by them.

The center has its own teaching-administrative staff, chosen in terms of the central mission of the institution. Each member is presumed to possess a mastery of the necessary subject-matter, a commitment to the ideal of residential continuing education, and a personality which can fulfil itself harmoniously in the intimate life of the center. Part-time teachers, carefully chosen, are also required, but the permanent staff provides the nucleus of the instructional program. The director of the center is its key figure. The Danish Vorstander does in fact stand in front, as his title implies,

---

[1] Quoted in: Peter E. Siegle, "The International Conference on Residential Adult Education: An Interpretive Review," Adult Education, VI (Winter, 1956), p. 107.

and is not merely first among equals. In the more traditional schools, people remain standing until he is seated, he is served first at meals, and, in countless direct or subtle ways, he makes it clear that he is the symbolic embodiment of the entire institution. The same ascendancy is true in other countries as well, though its manifestations depend on the national character. In England, for example, the director may affect a certain modest self-deprecation and diffidence, but everybody is aware that, as Rogers put it in describing one center, "There is only one conference going on at a time and one man is always in charge."[1]

The center has a separate identity of its own. It should be set apart either geographically or in some symbolic way so that the residential quality of the learning experience may be stressed. Many European centers are placed in settings of beautiful natural surroundings in the countryside or in their own parks, while others occupy distinctive buildings in urban locations. Both are separate from other structures and functions-and that separateness is stressed. The accommodations provided, particularly bedrooms and meals, may be frugal and Spartan. They are not as bare, cold, and dark as the early Danish models, but the concept of "plain living and high thinking" is clearly embodied within them. Thus, the comforts and privacy of home are stripped away so that the individual can be made more quickly responsive than he would be otherwise to the educative impact of communal living.

Each conference is composed of a small enough group so that everyone may establish his own identity within it. Each person is recognized as an individual, rather than as an anonymous member of the group, and takes his place as an integral part of its social composition. He may have come to the conference in a mood of suspicious withholding of self or with a determination to survey the situation carefully before committing himself in any way. He quickly abandons that view, not only because of the constant day-long

---

[1]William C. Rogers, "Wilton Park: International Conference Champion?" The NUEA Spectator, XXXIV (April-May, 1969), p. 21.

association with others but also because his unique background and experience become resources on which he can draw to contribute to both formal and informal discussion. "Living together," says Guy Hunter, the English author, "produces a relaxation of barriers which makes adult education ten times easier."[1] The small conference helps each individual who comes to it to establish his own identity in the eyes of others and often himself.

The center fosters a sense of community which leads the individual to enlarge his knowledge of others and of himself in relation to others. Teachers and students live together in informal circumstances and each group thus formed soon develops its unique characteristics. The task of everyone (but especially of the staff) is to be sure that these characteristics are as favorable as possible to the reinforcement of learning. Outlooks are broadened, new human relationships are formed, and everyone concerned gains a heightened sense of the values of other individuals as they interact with his own. The socialization process which does so much to shape human personality has its customary effect and, in the words of Laurence Speak, the sense of fellowship can be "the bridge to a new outlook on society, and more than an outlook, a new feeling for the community."[2]

This value is fostered because the conference provides a complete break from the normal processes of life of those who come to it. They are detached from the routines of work, home, and social life, and from the other reinforcements of the stereotyped viewpoints which adults may acquire as they move along their accustomed pathways. The demands of one's occupation and expectations of all the other people with whom one interacts are removed, resulting in a sense of liberation. Such freedom, while probably welcome to most people, also presents psychological threats to them. Suddenly there is a

---

[1]Quoted in: Robert H. Schacht, Week-end Learning in the U.S.A Chicago: Center for the Study of Liberal Education for Adults, 1960), p. 4.

[2]Ibid., p. 294.

17

new perspective: on one's self, on one's customary associates and associations, and on society as a whole. The learning which occurs under such circumstances is bound to be different from that sandwiched in among life's normal experiences. Some people are too set in their ways to be jarred loose even by the most profound residential learning experience but, for most of those who attend, some break with routinized thought occurs. At the maximum, the life of the individual and his effect on society may be transformed - as often results, Arnold Toynbee says, from "the temporary withdrawal of the creative personality from his social milieu and his subsequent return to the same milieu transfigured in a new capacity with new powers."[1]

This break is made more pronounced by the fact that the purpose of the center is wholly educational. The values of full-time community can be secured in many ways: on cruises, in holiday camps, on club outings, or on conducted tours. In a European residential center such values are fostered not for themselves alone but for their long-range educational impact. The staff of a center may be as interested in recreation as a cruise director, but the reason for that interest is wholly different in the two cases and (if the program is successful) so is the effect. The completeness of the educative purpose is intended to have a profound influence on the participant. For him, planned learning becomes central, not peripheral, intermittent, or non-existent. The whole day may be spent in moving forward to new horizons. The very openness of the situation frightens or frustrates some people; they seek trivial things to do, manufacture obstacles, enter into conflict with others, withdraw psychologically, or use any of the other retreats from thought open to them. But most conference participants rise to the challenge; they adjust to the full-time learning situation and are exhilarated by the unaccustomed continuing exercise of their minds. They have direct personal experience, sometimes for the first time in their adulthood, of what sustained intellectual life can be. And, for at least a

---

[1]Quoted in Schacht, Weekend Learning, p. 2.

18

few, the end-result man be a reordering of their personal priorities and
a replanning of their future.

The techniques used to achieve the educational purpose rely heavily on
the processes of direct oral communication. Discussions, lectures,
question-and-answers, symposia, panels, demonstrations, conducted
explorations: these are the formal means of teaching and learning, supported
always by the continuing interaction of communal living. At a conference,
there can be relatively little time for reading, writing, introspection, or
other solitary pursuits; they should occur, if at all, as preparation or as
follow-up, leaving the scarce time of the shared experience for human interaction. This process can be viewed too narrowly. The "living word" of
Grundtvig has been debased in some European residential centers by the
tendency of their leaders to give interminable lectures or in other ways to
adopt the master-and-disciples posture in which they speak with an air of
infallibility - "because I say it, it is so." But occasional excess does not
destroy the validity of Cardinal Newman's contention that when men and
women

> aim at something precise, something refined, something really
> luminous, something really large, something choice . . . they
> avail themselves, in some shape or other, of . . . the ancient
> method, of oral instruction, of present communication between
> man and man, of teachers instead of teaching, of the personal
> influence of a master, and the humble initiation of a disciple . . .
> if we wish to become exact and fully furnished in any subject of
> teaching which is diversified and complicated, we must consult
> the living man and listen to his living voice.[1]

Whatever may be the specific aim of a conference or of a center, the
participants in residential adult education are expected to become better
citizens of their nation and of the world. As the Dutch authority, Oscar
Guermonprez put it, "The education of the individual should be so designed
as to provide him with a sense of responsibility toward the wider community."[2]

---

[1] John Henry Newman, University Sketches (Dublin: Browne and Nolan,
Ltd., Undated. Text of 1856), pp. 7-8.

[2] In Siegle, "The International Conference," p. 107.

19

This end may be sought by helping an individual learn how to play one of his social roles, such as elected official, union member or officer, or church leader, or by devoting part of the program to national or international issues. Informally, all the elements of the social setting may be devised to help build responsibility and a sense of cohesiveness. Among the processes used to achieve this purpose are: group singing, the elevation of ritualistic procedures into institutional traditions, the creation of steering committees or some other form of collective decision-making, the use of participants in program leadership posts, organized recreation and tours, and the provision of a bar. While all such activities are adjuncts of the program, their importance is defended by the leaders of European residential education.

* * *

The total ethos of that education is suggested by the elements identified above, but there is still plenty of room for intense factionalism which tends to be based not on form but on purpose. The leaders of European centers represent the full political-economic spectrum from communism to a reactionary point of view; they may be bitterly split on rural-urban issues; in Denmark, the "inner light" schools which express religious fundamentalism are set apart from the more secular schools; and many other bases of difference exist. Nor does the identification of either general or special ideals mean that their achievement is guaranteed. A center may profess all of them but, without strong, informed, and practiced leadership, it may become simply a place where its participants can have a cheap vacation with little effort. One English author, attacking the actual achievement of the centers of his country, noted ironically:

> Perhaps in the end it is all a matter of inertia, with a strong
> dash of nostalgia. The memory of those long, sunny, summer
> afternoons at Salisbury, the easy drone which allowed one's
> eyes and mind to stray out across the dreaming spires at that
> good weekend at Oxford, the handy pitch-and-putt next to the
> hotel at Fleetwood - with a little mild entertainment in the
> morning, gentle recreation for the afternoon and a good bar for

the evening - what more could anyone want?[1]

The answer seems to be that people want much more - and it is the effort both to fulfill their desires and to achieve the aspirations of the leaders of residential continuing education that has guided the European centers during the course of their century - long development.

---

[1] Arthur Stock, "A Time to Confer?" Adult Education [British], XLI (September, 1968), p. 154.

III. THE AMERICAN EXPERIENCE

The American patterns of residential continuing education are larger,
more fluid, and more open than those of Europe. Some transfer of institutions and practices has been made from the old world to the new, and the
latter has repaid the debt by creating ideas and institutions which Europe
could borrow, as when English universities adopted the summer school or
when three young Americans founded Ruskin College at Oxford. The
century-long experience of the United States with both indigenous and
borrowed patterns will only be sketched here to provide a background for
an account of the growth of university centers for residential continuing
education in the middle third of the twentieth century.

Attempts to Transfer the European Conception

In the United States, the European conception of residential adult
education has had a long tradition and many adherents. A constant stream
of migrants and of American voyagers returning from abroad has brought
the idea to this country, and many institutions have been created or influenced thereby, but the European conception has achieved neither unity as
a movement nor profound impact on the nation's life and education.

At least three efforts have been made to create such a movement: (1)
The Scandinavians who came to this country (particularly to Minnesota,
Nebraska, and nearby states) tried to import the folk high school intact.
Grundtvig's son was one such person, helping to prepare the way for the
best-known such center, Danebod, at Elk Horn, Iowa. There were others
as well - but none of them thrived. (2) In the Appalachian highlands, many
efforts were made to help local inhabitants learn to improve their lot
in life through education, and the idea of the folk high school was adapted
in many ways. One well-known institution was founded by Olive Campbell,
who wrote a book on the Danish system and who did much to help develop
the crafts of the mountain people. Other schools, most notably the Highlander

Folk School, addressed themselves to questions of economics and race and launched attacks on prejudice and inequality. (3) In the 1950's and 1960's, a number of Americans rediscovered the European ideas (as they had been developed by that time in many countries) and created a section of the Adult Education Association to promote their vision of what residential adult education might be. Among these influential leaders were Philip Klein, Royce Pitkin, Robert Schacht, Peter Siegle, and Robert Ulich.

Indigenous American Patterns

The fostering of the European tradition, however, has been a relatively small strand of development, surrounded and engulfed by countless other ventures. Among the most important were these:

1. The religiously-oriented camp meeting or retreat. Chautauqua Institution, founded in 1874, became almost instantly famous as a summer-long center for religious, literary, and artistic study, and its example was soon followed, all over the country, by other places of a similar sort. Nobody knows the total in existence, but they still serve vast populations and many have extended their programs to provide year-round conferences and retreats.[1]

2. The agricultural short course. In the great effort to teach American farmers to use scientific techniques, one of the chief methods was to bring them together to study some specific process for a short period of time, most frequently on the campus of a land-grant college. Out of these specialized ventures, there gradually developed general "farmers' weeks," provided each year to large numbers of people. Both were important in bringing about the agrarian revolution which changed the nature of American rural life and helped provide the political backing which enables "cow colleges" to develop into comprehensive universities. While some vestiges

---

[1] The Roman Catholic tradition of the religious retreat is especially long and deep. For an account of its essentials, see: Thomas C. Hennessy, S. J., editor, The Inner Crusade: The Closed Retreat in the United States (Chicago: Loyola University Press, 1965).

of this form of residential continuing education remain, it has largely been absorbed by broader programs of service to rural America.

3. The university summer session. Following the example set by Chautauqua, American universities began in the last quarter of the nineteenth century to offer special courses in the summer time. Their central mission was to provide in-service training for the teachers of the rapidly burgeoning schools of the country, though efforts were made to reach other groups of adults as well. The summer session has gradually become an integral part of the general academic offering, but short-term courses, institutes, and workshops are still offered during the summer at many colleges and universities.

4. Conventions and conferences. As the economic and political life of the country grew in size and complexity, more and more efforts have been made to bring people together periodically for industrial, commerical, governmental, associational, and special-interest gatherings. Some are purely educational; others mix learning or informational aims with recreation, fraternization, the transaction of business, the sponsorship of legislation, and other purposes. But whatever the special form, the convention and the conference have become established parts of modern American life and reach countless people every year.

These varied forms and patterns are not harmonized by any coherent body of opinion or discourse. The religiously-oriented centers go their separate ways and the agricultural courses have merged into the general offerings of the university extension service. An association of summer session deans is in existence, but it does not exercise strong national leadership. In addition, the provision of conventions and conferences is so large and diffuse that little effort is made to grasp its scope and meaning. A vast literature exists, but it deals largely with descriptive and practical topics;[1]

---

[1]Examples of such books are: Richard Beckhard, How to Plan and Conduct Workshops and Conferences (New York: Association Press, 1956); Herbert S. Kindler, Organizing the Technical Conference (New York: Reinhold Publishing Corporation, 1960); and Harry P. Zelko, The Business Conference (New York: MrGraw-Hill Book Company, 1969).

no body of continuing discussion and writing has shaped and focused the overall conceptions of residential continuing education.

The closest approximation to an American movement began to emerge
in the 1920's and 1930's. American universities had long been directly or
indirectly influenced by the various forms of residential continuing education,
first with the summer session and the agricultural short course, then with
other applications of the idea. In the beginning, the full responsibility for
an activity rested with a single faculty member or administrator, but as the
volume of service increased, special "conferences and institutes" offices
were created to handle the details of operation. The people who manned
such offices began to appear in increasing numbers at the gatherings of the
National University Extension Association.

In the 1930's, at least two universities took the logical next step by
establishing physical facilities to house conferences. The first, the
University of Florida, began in October, 1936 to operate Camp Roosevelt,
a converted construction headquarters lent from the U.S. Department of
Engineers. Of greater eventual significance, however, was the Center for
Continuation Study, opened a month later at the University of Minnesota,
for it was the first university-sponsored building especially designed and
constructed for residential continuing education. While the example of the
folk high school was much in the minds of the Scandinavian-descended
Minnesotans, the primary purpose of the new center was to provide continuing
education for members of various professions. The Florida center did not
long survive, and the Minnesota center was relinquished by the university
to the army during World War II, but the two early ventures had attracted
sufficient attention to cause many other universities to ponder the possible
significance for themselves of the new form of residential continuing
education.

Between 1945 and 1950, this interest took several forms. The
University of Oklahoma converted the buildings of a nearby Navy cantonment
area into a center. Syracuse University and the University of Illinois
pioneered in a different form of center, a mansion converted into a place for
residential learning; it resembled the institutions created after World War

II in England. A national survey in 1949 of the program aspirations of extension deans showed that they placed the creation of a center at the top of their priority lists. And the interest of the National University Extension Association was crystallized when, at its 1949 meeting, the first special session was held for the administrators of conferences and institutes.

The major event of that period, however, was the collaboration of the W. K. Kellogg Foundation and Michigan State University (then called Michigan State College) in the series of events culminated by the opening of the W. K. Kellogg Center for Continuing Education in 1951. Both institutions had gained a great deal of experience with conferences. A major responsibility of the Foundation in the 1930's and 1940's had been to improve the quality of life in seven counties near its headquarters in Battle Creek; in fulfilling this mission, local citizens were provided with week-long workshops on university campuses and at Foundation-operated camps. These experiences caused Foundation officials to acquire a high esteem for this form of learning. The University had pioneered the agricultural short course movement, had sponsored an annual Farmers' Week, had maintained a summer session, and had experimented with other forms of residential learning. The University was also interested in developing a special program in hotel management and needed a practice facility to use for that purpose. Thus, both tradition and current interest had prepared the two institutions for innovations.

Three men took the leadership in this venture. One was W. K. Kellogg himself. He was deeply concerned with the improvement of the lot of mankind and intended his money to be used for this purpose. "Given opportunity and encouragement," he said, "people will use evolving ideas in health, education and recreation to insure that the new generation will have a better life than the old."[1] He was delighted with the thought that the new center could be a continuing instrument for this purpose. The second man

---

[1] "General Information Concerning the W. K. Kellogg Foundation." Issued by the Foundation, p. 3.

was Emory Morris, who was chief administrative officer of the Foundation from 1943 to 1970. He not only helped to shape the ideas for the Kellogg Center but was later concerned with the development of other institutions of the same sort. The third man, John Hannah, President of Michigan State College, believed strongly in the importance of residential study, and saw clearly how a center would help in that endeavor. In his proposal to the Foundation, he wrote:

> Our experience has indicated the great value of these short courses and conferences. The men and women who come in from their farms or businesses and devote a few days or a few weeks to study on the campus almost invariably return to the communities from which they come and put into practice the ideas and inspirations that were gained here. They are able to see a direct and almost immediate return from the advantages of the additional education and are most appreciative of it.

But while these three gave overall guidance and direction to the development of the Kellogg Center, it was Maurice Seay who shaped its central theme and purpose and worked out the design to achieve them. He had become deeply involved in adult education as Chief of the Education and Training Division of the Tennessee Valley Authority during its formative years when it was changing the economic and cultural patterns of the mid-South. This experience showed him how the knowledge produced by research might be used to provide a richer and more rewarding life for mankind, and most of his later career has been devoted to the search for new ways of bringing about that result.

His special concern with residential continuing education began when he served from 1944 to 1950 as a member of the Advisory Committee on Education of the Kellogg Foundation. In 1948-49, he took a leave from the University of Kentucky to aid Presdent Hannah in the development of the plan for the Kellogg Center. Later, from 1954 to 1964, he served as the Director of the Division of Education of the Foundation. It was during this period that most of the Kellogg-sponsored centers were begun, and it was Seay who shaped and guided their growth into a nation-wide movement.

Many universities asked the Foundation to support their work in residential continuing education; for example, fifty-three formal proposals were received between 1957 and 1961. The awards made followed a logical and coherent plan set forth in a document by Seay and called "The Fifteen Criteria."[1]

The Kellogg Center as it finally evolved at Michigan State was essentially a new kind of institution, even though it embodied many ideas and patterns drwan from precursor programs. Its guiding theme was to apply the advanced knowledge of university faculty members to the direct improvement of human life and, in the process, to bring the concerns of man and his society to the attention of scholars and researchers. Ideally, the entire faculty would eventually be put in touch with the entire society. To achieve this purpose, the building and its services were complex. It was a 24-hour-a-day, 365-days-a-year facility complete with all services required for education in a self-contained community. It was large enough to hold a variety of programs operating simultaneously and it had a staff to guide programs and provide supportive services. In largeness of conception and complexity of operation, the center was unique.

It was not to retain this position very long, however, for success led to many imitators. The Foundation itself has now aided in the creation of nine additional centers, eight in the United States and one at Oxford in England. They take varied forms and have many specific purposes, but all have the same essential mission as the Kellogg Center. This programmatic purpose expressed the concern felt by Seay and his colleagues, who have always considered the buildings to be instruments for social advance, significant only as they made possible a complex and continuing flow of new ways to apply the knowledge of the specialist to the service of mankind.

The movement thus stimulated by the Foundation has now grown

---

[1] Harold J. Alford, Continuing Education in Action (New York: John Wiley and Sons, Inc., 1968), pp. 23-27. This book is an account of the nature and growth of the Kellogg-sponsored centers.

to substantial size. In a study[1] completed in August, 1968, Ann Litchfield was able to identify 118 centers in the United States and 32 in Canada. Of the 118 centers, 86 were university-sponsored, almost equally divided between those on campus and those off. The number of university centers founded each year has gradually increased; in the 1950s, two or three new ones appeared each year, but in the 1960s, the annual increase was from four to nine. These institutions vary greatly in size, scope, and purpose, but collectively their work represents a major new force in continuing residential education.

Essentials of the American Conception

Amidst all the diversity of the indigenous American experience with residential learning, the university-based centers represent the clearest and most coherent strand of development. Their purposes and nature will be explored in some depth in a later section of this essay. Before turning to this topic, however, it may be useful to contrast the earlier analysis of the European conception of continuing education with a similar analysis of practice in the United States. The size, diversity, and fluidity of the American offering make such a task difficult, but certain tentative generalizations can nonetheless be suggested. They are focused on university-oriented practice because most of the available literature describes it, but they also deal in some fashion with the whole American practice of residential continuing education.

To begin with, residential continuing education in the United States is massive in size and growing rapidly. Nobody can say how many conferences are held each year, partly because they have so many different sponsors and partly because they shade off so imperceptibly into conventions, sales promotion gatherings, management meetings, equipment shows, and other

---

[1] A Directory of Residential Continuing Education Centers. Report by the Studies and Training Program in Continuing Education, The University of Chicago, 1968.

kinds of activity. The best available data are those of the member institutions of the National University Extension Association and the Association of University Evening Colleges. In 1960-61 they provided 6,685 conferences enrolling 713,000 people; by 1969-70, the figure had risen to 21,458 conferences with 1,698,218 registrants.[1]

Residential continuing education is conducted in many kinds of settings and is not distinctively an activity of special centers established for the purpose. While the number of such centers is growing, organized conferences are also held in many other kinds of facilities, among them hotels, motels, university residence halls, summer encampments, and private homes. This fact is also true in Europe, but non-center conferences there are likely not to be considered part of residential continuing education.

The special centers for residential education tend to be complex, multi-purpose, and well equipped with amenities. In a few cases, an American center is dominated by a single purpose, usually religious in nature, but, for the most part, goals inhere in the individual conferences, not in the facility itself. Many centers are designed to house simultaneously several conferences which may vary widely in their objective. In earlier days, new centers were designed by their architects to look like hotels, hospitals, or dormitories, but today they are evolving uniquely functional forms of their own. Americans who go to conferences expect a high standard of services and facilities: confortable rooms, private baths, maid service, excellent food, and good recreational facilities. As a result, some of the American centers seem almost obscenely magnificent to all those who believe in the doctrine of plain living and high thinking, or who worry about the denial of opportunities to those who cannot afford the high

---

[1] These and other NUEA-AUEC figures to be given later have been assembled from various statistical reports issued by the two organizations. It should be noted that many universities which sponsor conferences belong to neither organization. Thirty-five percent of the centers identified by Litchfield were in such universities.

prices which the centers must charge. On no other point is there so much criticism of American residential education, partly by foreigners, partly by Americans themselves. Writing in 1955, before the program of the W. K. Kellogg Foundation was well under way, Royce Pitkin observed that "it would be quite unfortunate if some generous legislature or philanthropist, seeing in the residential adult school a means for a great educational crusade, were to establish a few huge hotel-like structures and call them residential schools. Though such hostelries might serve usefully as convention centers and meeting places for citizens, they would lack the intimate homely characteristics of the genuine educational institutions. "[1] Thirteen years later, Robert Blakely called such centers "Hilton-Taj Mahals" and said,"in my judgment the building of large, elaborate, expensive centers for continuing education has harmed the development of university conferences. "[2]

The focus of American residential education is not upon the development of man as a whole being but upon his capacity to discharge his several roles. Education for liberal pursuits is far from unknown in this country, but it is not a central emphasis of the American tradition. Because the customary purpose of a conference is to deal with some personal or social problem, the range of persons involved in it tends to be limited to a relatively homogenous group. But since the number of conferences is so very great, collectively they reach out broadly into many realms of knowledge. The subject-matter breakdown of NUEA-AUEC conferences in 1969-70 was:

agriculture	8.9%
behavior sciences	6.5%

---

[1]Royce Pitkin, "The Case for the Residential Idea in Adult Education" (unpublished address given at the Annual Conference of the Adult Education Association, St. Louis, Missouri, November 13, 1955), pp. 23-24.

[2]Robert Blakely, "How Does Short Term Learning Fulfill Societal Needs," N.U.E.A. Spectator, XXX (February-March 1968), pp. 12-13.

biological sciences	1.2%
business	10.4%
education	18.3%
engineering	5.5%
health professions	8.6%
humanities	10.6%
law	4.4%
physical sciences	2.3%
interdisciplinary	10.4%
other	12.9%

The Americans tend to accept and plan for several   basically different kinds of short residential learning experiences. Several conference forms are widely used. Later in the essay a complex typology will be presented, but the most commonly recognized patterns are: the short course, in which one or more leaders teach well-established knowledge to the partici-pants; the programmed conference, in which a series of varied learning experiences is provided for the benefit of a specific group of participants; the exploratory conference, where people with different views try to work out areas of agreement or come to understand one another better; and the problem-solving conference where policies are shaped on the basis of discussion.[1] All of these kinds of conferences - and others as well - occur in both Europe and the United States, though it is likely that the short course is most common in the former and the programmed conference is most common in the latter. But the difference among the various types and the need for considering each one separately is more widely understood among the Americans than among the Europeans, though a comparative consideration of the various forms is marred in both places by a tendency

---

[1]The short course and the programmed conference are well understood, at least in their essential forms, but the following references may be useful to anyone who would like to know more about the less commonly-found forms or short-term learning: Mary Capes, editor, Communication or Conflict (New York: Association Press, 1960); Frank Fremont-Smith, "The Inter-disciplinary Conference," AIBS Bulletin (April, 1961), pp. 17-20, 32; and George B. Thomas, "Learning at a Conference," Phi Delta Kappan (April, 1968), pp. 447-448.

to regard some one type of conference as being inherently the best or, indeed, as being the only true form.

One reason why the diversity of conference types tends to be stressed in the United States is because conference staffs and analysts have great interest in process and technique. In other countries, there is a tendency to celebrate the purposes or the specific values of a center or of its conference and to take the means pretty much for granted. Here there is a tendency to accept the values as obvious and to concentrate on the designing of the learning experience and the perfection of its component parts. Both Europeans and Americans sometimes become doctrinaire and try to impose Freudian, Lewinian, or other theories on the conference form. For the most part, however, the American concern with conference planning is expressed in an effort to consider carefully each step in the educative process as it stretches from pre-planning through follow-up to see that every stage of operation is suitably designed and conducted.

In the United States, the people centrally concerned with conference operation are administrators who leave the direct teaching to other people usually chosen for that purpose on a part-time basis. Full-time instructors are almost always part of the staffs of European centers; they are almost never part of the staffs of American centers, though in some cases (as at the University of Georgia and the University of Maryland) some faculty members may have special responsibility for designing conferences. In the United States, teaching is done by many people but it is integrated and made meaningful by the work of "co-ordinators," the most common American term for staff members of residential centers. At this work, Rogers affirms, "most agree it is hard to beat the experience of the old hands in the business who are usually in the well established state universities."[1]

Unlike much American adult education, residential learning is undertaken to achieve a variety of personal and social goals rather than for the purpose of securing formal credits and degrees. Various pressures or

---

[1] Rogers, "Wilton Park," p. 20.

33

even compulsions reinforce attendance at many conferences, such as those sponsored by industry, but the need to meet the formal standards of youth-based schooling are far less evident in residential education than in other kinds of institutional adult learning. In 1969-70, for example, only 8.6% of the correspondence course registrations and 13.1% of the extension class registrations in NUEA-AUEC universities were non-credit, whereas 97.7% of the conference registrations fell into that category. Other institutions which sponsor conferences are even less likely than the university to award degrees, credits, and other forms of certification.

As residential education expands in size and scope, it is tending to become a part of a continuing or recurrent life-style rather than a separate and isolated experience. Americans tend increasingly to combine study with recreation and make it a part of a family experience. Many centers, such as those at Chautauqua and Aspen, are established on this basis, and others go to some lengths to welcome and provide activities for the families of participant-students. Many motels and resorts are successful in attracting conferences because they can provide facilities for the non-conferees who come along. Some conference leaders deplore this reduction in the purity of the educational motive, but resign themselves to accepting it on the half-a-loaf-is-better-than-none rationale. Other conference leaders feel that the mixing of purposes adds strength to each. As Schacht says, " In this age in which so many factors operate to pull families apart, there may be considerable value in offering residential experiences which bring families together with other families. "[1]

Contrast and Collaboration

To contrast the two sets of propositions concerning European and American residential continuing education is to perceive that the first deals with the definition and embodiment of one ideal, while the second has

----

[1]Schacht, Week-End Learning, p. 13.

to do with description of the implementation of a distinctive form of learning characterized by many ideals and likely to add more. The two ways of thought can be divisive. As noted earlier, some Englishmen exclude from their thought about residential continuing education the work of centers primarily concerned with occupational training; such centers should exist, of course, but on some different plane than the others; they are simply not "what is meant in this country by residential adult education." An American has difficulty grasping or accepting the point. On the other hand, some Americans seem to think that merely by designing and building a conference as meticulously as a Swiss watchmaker undertakes his craft, it is sure to be a success; the worthiness of the purpose itself, the need for significant content, the advantage of having a single integrative personality in charge, or the desirability of creating a collective ethos may be ignored. A European has difficulty grasping or accepting the point. But the two ways of thought can be complementary and, as we noted above, both the Europeans and the Americans have long borrowed ideas and practices from one another.

More important, they have collaborated in the analysis of the significance of conference activities and manifestations. The number of international and intranational conferences has grown so great since the end of World War II and has involved so many social analysts of all sorts that a literature of conference sociology has grown up. Its fullest expression is found in the book Communication or Conflict, edited by Mary Capes, which reports the highlights of an "international conference on the process and functioning of international conferences."[1] Here a group of specialists from several countries and from many disciplines (including psychiatry, public health, industrial management, anthropology, and education) listened to a few papers but, more important, set about the task of analyzing in detail the practical aspects and problems of conference operation. The procedure

---

[1] Capes, Communication or Conflict, p. ix.

was wholly inductive. There was no effort to interpret into practice the key principles of a Grundtvig or a Livingstone; instead the conferees examined the realities of residential continuing education in an effort to find uniformities of style and practice and good rules to follow.

Margaret Mead has paid close attention in many of her works to the customs and habitual behavior of conference participants. She contributed the major paper in Communication or Conflict, and (with Paul Byers) she wrote The Small Conference: An Innovation in Communication.[1] No detail is too small for her attention. She sums up a lengthy discussion of the relevance of alchololic beverages by concluding that "It may be taken as a general rule that drinks should be available on the premises." Food is important, particularly for those with special diets. "There should be choice allowed of foods that occur in a simple state, like fruit or nuts, to comfort the stranger who finds the local food difficult." People need to escape from general sessions into privacy and intimate conversation tion. "One large overlighted living room where everyone is in full view of everyone else all evening can nullify the success of the previous conference session."[2]

She reports such rules not merely as empirical bits of advice, but because she sees behind them some deep-seated realities of human behavior which come to the fore in the conference situation. Thus, for many people, a conference becomes a contradiction between overt and covert beliefs:

> Conferences may release deep-seated and unacknowledged ambivalences and deeply buried and disallowed attitudes. As all such conferences are by definition based on a kind of diversity which involves crossing boundaries, one of the common motives for participation is a belief on the part of the participant that crossing boundaries - between disciplines or the sexes, or age groups, or organizational

---

[1]Margaret Mead and Paul Byers, The Small Conference: An Innovation in Communication (Paris: Mouton and Co., 1968).

[2]Margaret Mead, "Conference Behavior," Columbia University Forum, X (Summer, 1967), p. 18.

> levels, between races or nations or ideologies - is a
> good thing. This consciously held ideal, however, may
> mask other attitudes, a strong sense of superiority of
> his own group, a deep envy of another group, a hostility
> toward his own group. And these deeper attitudes may
> be released in the multi-sensory, many-to-many inter-
> change of a conference. [1]

Such conflicts can be resolved or at least contained by good conference procedure, and that is why both observation of processes and their evaluation
are so important. Long-run behavior is also influenced because, through
recurrent attendance at good conferences, people learn how to behave at
them. Thus Miss Mead describes one conference in the United Kingdom
which violated every rule of desirable procedure yet somehow managed to
be "a good conference." How was this possible? The only feasible answer
seemed to be that "the participants had incorporated the good arrangements
of previous conferences and worked within an imaginary set of conditions that
did not obtain at this particular one. "[2]

Miss Mead's greatest contribution to the literature of the conference
comes from her establishment of its importance in the education of even the
keenest intellects of our society and from her recognition that when such
intellects congregate to learn from each other, they must follow accepted
rules of good procedure. They are not above the laws of learning, though
they sometimes talk and act as though they were. For her, the conference
and its allied forms of communication have an ultimately social value. They
make possible truly creative growth in our society because they provide for
"the intercommunicating group of human beings who stand at some crucial
point of divergence in a process of culture change. "[3]

---

[1] Ibid., p. 19.

[2] Ibid., p. 18.

[3] Margaret Mead, Continuities in Cultural Evolution (New Haven: Yale
University Press, 1964) , p. xviii.

IV. THE UNIVERSITY-BASED CENTER

Now it is time to narrow the focus to look directly at the university-based center as it has emerged as an institutional form in the United States. While many of the following observations may apply to off-campus centers or even to non-building-based conference and institute programs, the chief frame of reference is the large complex on-campus center, of which there are today probably between forty or fifty examples. What are the prime purposes of a center? How are they discharged? What is the place of the center in the overall structure and prestige systems of the university? The balance of this essay will be devoted to an effort to answer these questions.

The Three Functions of the Center

Every center, if it is to be most meaningfully educative, must link itself in complex ways to the fundamental work of the university: teaching and research. In this respect, it is but another expression of that grand sweep of extension services that Jacques Maritain has called "one of the finest achievements of American education."[1] What is true of a residential center is, to some degree, also true of other forms of service, such as extension centers, correspondence study, radio and television programming, and agricultural and home economics extension. Today the university is increasingly serving the adults of its society, and such service has common elements in whatever form it is provided.

But a center also has special characteristics. Many university faculty members are involved in its work, sometimes in a teaching role but often as participants; conferences are one of the chief ways by which academic people enlarge their own understanding. Because conferences tend to be

---

[1] Jacques Maritain, Education at the Crossroads (New Haven: Yale University Press, 1943), p. 83.

brief, they are able to attract many people who could not otherwise spare the time; because conferences are intensive, they are capable of a powerful impact. If a separate building exists, its creation has usually been brought about by concentrated efforts of the governing board, the president, and the deans, who are all therefore somewhat informed about its potential. The overhead cost is substantial, rendering the success of its program a matter of both educational and financial concern. Some of its activities are high-prestige events, often involving distinguished outside leaders. If the center is on the campus, it serves as a continuing presence, usually an attractive one; it may become a focus of campus life. Moreover,the participants at campus conferences are more highly visible at the university itself than the correspondence or extension class students. If the conference is away from the campus, it is often in an attractive retreat, offering the possibility of a desirable setting, without distractions,which will encourage the building of a community of feeling and thought.

What contributions, then, can the center for continuing education make as an integral part of a university? What values can be derived from its use by the community of scholars whose work is at the heart of the institution's purposes?

One answer (the most clear and obvious) is that it provides a major instrument for teaching adults.

A second answer, increasingly given, is that it will furnish an important means for training leaders of the adult educational movement. A survey conducted several years ago by the National Opinion Research Center showed that about twenty-five million American adults were then systematically engaged in studying either independently or as registrants in various community institutions.[1] For the most part, the leaders of these institutions have acquired their skills by apprenticeship or by trial-and-error. As the number

---

[1]John W. C. Johnstone and Ramon J. Rivera, Volunteers for Learning (Chicago: Aldine Publishing Company, 1965), p. 38.

of adults interested in education grows and the need to develop sophisticated service becomes apparent, the leaders of the various institutions must have more adequate and efficient methods of preparation for their responsibilities. The centers of residential continuing education can provide valuable help in this respect, as well as offering various kinds of training and observation for other groups.

A third answer (one of great potential significance) is that these centers may serve as the foci or the sites of research in adult education, sociology, psychology, human development, and allied fields. This investigation can occur at a number of different levels. Simple service studies may deal with the improvement of practices. More sustained research efforts may be devoted to the testing of general principles or models by focusing either on the conference as an educative experience or upon the participants as learners. It is even conceivable that general theoretical investigations of major importance can emerge from and be tested by the multiplex activities of the residential centers.

Before turning to a detailed analysis of these three purposes as they are sought simultaneously in a center for continuing residential education, it may be useful to inquire whether parallels are to be found in other parts of the university's activity. In various ways a center is dissimilar to a department, a school, an experiment station, or any other unit which concentrates on teaching or research. It also differs substantially from other extension services, though such services are perhaps homologous to it more than to other parts of the university. Are there, however, other sectors of university life which, in fact, embody the basic functions identified above?

Upon reflection, it is apparant that there are at least two: the laboratory school and the university hospital.

The first task of a laboratory school is to teach its students in the best way possible. In carrying out this assignment, its staff also explicitly accepts two other aims: the training of school teachers and administrators; and the conduct of studies and research. Even when the school is, in fact, not doing very much teacher-training or research, it ordinarily states that it is, because faculty members recognize that the triple functions give them their status as members of the community of scholars which makes up the university itself. Parents who send their children to such schools also accept the three purposes. They know that while the education of the children must be the school's first concern, it will be conducted in an atmosphere which fosters training and research and in settings designed and organized to make all three functions operative. Moreover, both the faculty and the parents ordinarily believe that each of the three purposes will be more fully achieved if all three are being simultaneously sought.

The first task of the <u>university hospital</u> is to heal its patients as efficiently as it can. But the education of doctors, nurses, and technicians (and, increasingly, the in-service education of all the health professions) is also an accepted function of such a hospital, as is its use for medical re-search. As with the laboratory school, the persons served recognize the importance of the triple purpose. Despite certain inconveniences for the patient, both he and the medical profession believe that the best hospital care is provided in a setting in which training and research are also undertaken.

The laboratory school and the teaching hospital, chiefly because they are anchored in specific academic units, are not exact parallels of the non-anchored center for residential continuing education. The resemblance is close enough, however, to suggest that the center may not achieve full stature as an integral part of the university until it can establish its own complex pattern of teaching, training, and research. The men and women who register for a conference have a right to expect excellent educative experience. The registrants must also learn to be prepared to accept the fact that a conference may be used for training purposes, and that they them-selves may be the subjects of research. This latter idea is as yet relatively novel, perhaps because universities have been so busy filling their centers with conferences and trying to make them truly educative that there has not been time to enunciate or carry out the other two functions. Nor do some

41

centers have staffs capable of sophisticated training or research. Those centers which have insisted on incorporating the second and third functions, however, have found that ordinarily they are well accepted by the participants, who are, on the whole, stimulated and made to feel important because their learning activities are studied and used for training.

The Teaching Function

The major task of a center is to provide a total environment for learning. Anyone who attends a conference comes into an unfamiliar setting away from customary supports and constraints. While elated by a warm, welcoming response from a staff member, he tends to become enraged by any rudeness encountered. He usually feels exposed and vulnerable, responding to every aspect of his new experience with heightened sensitivity. Margaret Mead has spoken with special feeling on this point:

> The conference room that is not cleaned in the morning, in which smoke of last night lingers over the table, the dreary meal in a dreary restaurant that precedes so many scientific meetings, the bad coffee or lukewarm cocoa that a meager and grudging budget provides, the equipment that is inadequate, that breaks down and is neither repaired nor replaced - these are the things that dampen not only the spirit but the imagination.[1]

The openness to stimuli of the conferees is an important aid to learning, constantly underlining the need for every staff member to understand and support the educational purpose of the conference.

"Intellectual advances," Miss Mead also commented, "have always taken place in settings that had an intrinsic style." If a center must be Spartan, then "everyone should be permitted to share in the acceptance of the Spartan fare, as a poor thing but their own." If a center is beautiful and well-equipped, the conferees can be challenged by its elegance and use its amenities and facilities with delight. "It is the sloppy, ineffective middle

---

[1]Mead, Continuities in Cultural Evolution, p. 315.

position that is intolerable." So far as it can, the staff - both program and supportive - should provide the care and the resources available to it, for it is the "small ext ra increments of challenge or delight that make the difference between stagnation and swiftly blossoming thought."[1]

While the total environment of a center can aid or hamper learning, the heart of its teaching function lies in the program itself. As previous usage has indicated, the basic instructional unit of residential continuing education is usually called a "conference," though other terms such as "institute," "short-courses," and "workshop" are sometimes used as substitutes or alternatives. As was also suggested earlier, American continuing residential education characteristically takes several forms. This fact is true of the university-based centers, where the word "conference" describes a genus of activities, not a species. Administrators have tended to classify their instructional units in several rough-and-ready ways. One is by source; conferences are said to be faculty-originated, center-originated, or community-originated. A second is by administrative continuity; there are "one-shot" spectaculars, perennial staples, and innovations which, if successful, may become staples. A third is by length, with various periods marked off, such as the one-day, the two-or three-day, and so forth. A fourth is by sponsorship: center-administered, university-administered, and outside-administered. Such classification schemes are useful for specific purposes, but none have been universally adopted and all of them deal only with some aspect of form, not with educational substance. In addition to these conferences, the physical facilities of the centers are also used for other meetings not arranged by the staff - such as administrative, faculty, or associational meetings. On the basis of a study of twelve centers in 1959, Carlson Crane estimated that about one-fourth of their activities fell into this category.[2] While such

---

[1]Ibid., p. 315.

[2]Carlson E. Crane, "A Critical Analysis of Selected University Continuing Education Centers in the United States" (unpubli shed doctoral thesis, New York University, 1959), pp. 104-05.

gatherings have undoubted educational significance, they are not considered, except incidently, in this essay.

A Taxonomic System: The only major effort to develop a classification system for forms of residential continuing education has been made by John Buskey, who studied the offerings at five university centers and inductively developed a taxonomy permitting the placement of virtually all of the 425 conferences for which he had adequat e data.   This classification is based on five program elements: objectives, patterns of interaction among participants, timing, kinds of participants, and degree of articulation of the components of the program.   The resulting typology is too complex to be included in its entirety here,but the twelve major types[1] are sketched briefly in Figure 1, p. 45

As yet this taxonomy is too new to have been widely used or tested in the field,but it (or some adaptation of it) may prove to be useful both for conference directors and researchers.   The former may be helped to clarify the aims of their programs and to achieve a meaningful overall description of the work of their centers.   The latter may be enabled to focus more directly than before on the specific kinds of conferences which they choose for analysis.

The Influence of Conferences on Their Participants: Despite the great growth of conference participation, some skeptics doubt their educational effectiveness, and comments like the one by Arthur Stock on an earlier page have been voiced by other people.   A conference can be enjoyable and atten- dance a refreshing experience but, when all is said and done, has anything really happened to the participants ?

Robert Florell explored this quest ion in a   study of the effect of six conferences at the University of Nebraska, which provided liberal, occupa- tional, functional, or recreational content.   The   Buskey taxonomy was not then available, but the conferences analyzed by Florell fell into several of his types, probably A-1, A-2, A13, and D-1.   The conferences were also

_____

[1] The wording of the twelve types used here adapts and greatly condenses that to be found in the original source: John H. Buskey, "The Development and Testing of a Typology of Adult Education Programs in University Resi- dential Centers" (unpublished doctoral dissertation, The University of Chicago, 1970).

Class A. The acquisition and comprehension of information and knowledge.

A-1. The dissemination of the latest information to experts in a field of study or a discipline.

A-2. The systematic presentation of a carefully defined body of basic knowledge to students who have a minimum of previous formal study.

A-3. The exploration or discussion of a problem by a general audience.

Class B. The application of knowledge to particular situations.

B-1. An instructional program in which the student acquires understanding of a body of basic knowledge and skills in applying that knowledge.

B-2. An organizational meeting whose purpose is to make decisions or solve problems having to do with the on-going activities or purposes of the organization.

B-3. The discussion or exploration of a problem with the goal of solving it by means of the discussions.

B-4. An intensive program in which individuals try to understand themselves and others better through the experience of interaction with other people.

Class C. The analysis or exploration of situations.

C-1. The analysis and discussion of social   or public issues by confrontation of knowledgeable participants who hold differing and often opposing views.

C-2. The systematic exploration and analysis of a problem or situation involving identification of the constituent elements or parts of the situation.

Class D. The synthesis or creation of plans or products.

D-1. The study of a discipline or field of study in order to organize it and derive a set of new questions or hypotheses for further research.

D-2. The creation of a plan or product by synthesizing or combining a number of elements into one integrated whole: a new curriculum, a plan for action, and so on.

Class E. The attempt to help the individual achieve the integration of personal values in one or more aspects of his life.

Figure 1.   The Buskey Typology of Conference Types

divided between those calling for the participant to apply what he had learned and those expecting him to influence others. In each case conferees were tested several weeks after the end of their conferences and their scores were compared with those of non-participants selected at random from the same general population. In every one of the six conferences, Florell found that the scores of the participants were significantly (p $<$ .01) higher than those of the non-participants.[1]

The Relative Effectiveness of Conferences and Other Program Formats: When residential continuing education began to appear prominently on the American scene, it added a new program format to those already in existence, such as courses, tutorial teaching, and independent study. The question naturally arose, therefore, as to whether a conference led to better educational outcomes than did the other formats. While a great deal of anecdotal evidence, pro and con, has been cited on this point, only three studies have yet dealt with it on a sophisticated basis. Each of the three selected an educational program which could be carried out in two or more formats, one being residential study. The conferences fall into several of Buskey's types. Various measures of accomplishment were used, ranging from a straightforward testing of the knowledge gained to complex and subtle measurements of personality change and interactive relationships. The results are far too complex to elaborate here, but in general it may be said that the conference stood up very well in comparison with the other formats used. In fact, where significant differences occurred, they were likely to favor the conference format as against the others.[2]

---

[1]Robert J. Florell, "Applicational Transfer in Adult Education" (unpublished doctoral dissertation, University of Nebraska, 1966).

[2]Norman W. Jackson, "An Exploratory Adult Education Program for Parents and Their Children of Senior High Age to Improve Communication in the Home" (unpublished doctoral thesis, Indiana University, 1964); A. A. Lacognata, "A Comparison of the Effectiveness of Adult Residential and Non-Residential Learning Situations," (Chicago: Center for the Study of Liberal Education of Adults, 1961); John H. Stevenson, "A Comparison Study of Residential and Non-Residential Adult Religious Educational Programs" (unpublished doctoral thesis, Indiana University, 1968).

<u>The Improvement of Conference Effectiveness</u>: A number of investigators have focused directly on the improvement of conferences, usually by studying some aspect of residential learning. For example, some conferences are planned collaboratively with participants or their representatives and others are not. Is such pre-planning (often very expensive and time-consuming) worthwhile? Eugene Welden studied this question by administering a specially devised conference evaluation form to 1,026 men and women who had attended 47 conferences at five university residential centers. This form was concerned with the affective rather than the cognitive results of the conferences. He found that those with participant planning were perceived by the conference attenders as more directly related to their personal motive than was the case in conferences planned without representation. Participants in the first group of conferences also had a significantly higher degree of satisfaction than did participants in the second group. On the other hand, participants in the first group did not express a higher degree of interest in continuing educative activity than did participants in the second group.[1]

James Kafka took the question of involvement one step further. Residential education has been said to have many advantages over other formats, but three most often mentioned are: a feeling of group isolation from external influences over a significant period of time; a capacity to confront directly a substantial body of content; and a sense of group support among the participants and staff. Kafka studied four conferences which varied in the extent to which they embodied these values. While the results were not significant in terms of the measurement of cognitive learning, the general trend of the data led Kafka to conclude that a conference in which a truly integrative educational experience exists is better than one in which it does not. In the latter, the three "advantages" might even turn out to have negative effects. He stressed the often-ignored truth that the mere fact of

---

[1]J. Eugene Welden, "Program Planning and Program Effectiveness in University Residential Centers" (unpublished doctoral dissertation, The University of Chicago, 1966).

residence is not necessarily a significant determinant of learning outcomes.[1]

The residential conference is generally recognized to be one of the most anxiety-producing of all educational formats. Observers of conferences have long believed that they reveal a common pattern of anxiety regardless of purpose, content, or length, but opinions have differed as to its nature. Some people have argued that it follows a lambda pattern (∧) with anxiety at its peak in the middle of the conference. Others have believed that it follows a V pattern with anxiety at its greatest at the beginning and the end. Ann Fales studied anxiety fluctuation in two conferences by administering to randomly selected samples of their participants each day the IPAT Anxiety Scale (which is a brief, disguised, easily scored, purportedly non-threatening instrument). She found that in both conferences, anxiety followed an M pattern, with average anxiety level being low at the beginning of the conferences, rising to a high point on the second day, dropping off on the third day, and rising again one day before the last day.[2]

The Assessment of a Center: Beyond such efforts to study the nature of various aspects of residential learning in order to strengthen the teaching function of the center lie broader questions of assessment which, while subjective, rest upon basic conceptions of the purpose of the university. Departments and services wax and wane in distinction; when a complex new form of university activity such as a residential continuing education center emerges on the scene, it too enters the cyclical pattern of growth and decline. While there are no established principles by which to judge the performance of university-based centers in terms of their excellence in teaching, at least six criteria have emerged from the extensive literature and discussion of recent years:

1. The program should be directed toward the achievement of significant educational purposes. Every university considers itself concerned with

---

[1]James J. Kafka, "Determinants of Residential Adult Education Effectiveness" (unpublished doctoral dissertation, The University of Chicago, 1970).

[2]Ann Wohlleben Fales, "Patterns of Anxiety in Residential Conferences," Continuing Education Report Number Eleven, The University of Chicago, 1966.

advanced and difficult subject matter rather than with elementary subjects, and with lofty purposes rather than pedestrian ones. Most universities, in addition, regard themselves as more powerful and influential than other educational institutions, with the actual or potential leaders of society as their natural clientele. If a center for continuing education wishes to establish its identification as a university service, therefore, its program must emphasize deeper rather than shallower bodies of content, must serve the professions rather than the trades, and must educate influential persons rather than those who carry little weight in the decisions of society. The center staff cannot and should not forget the needs of other adults in society, but it may be able to aid them best by putting on demonstration programs which other agencies might then adopt, or by collaborating with or stimulating other institutions (such as community colleges, public schools, or voluntary associations) to serve men and women on a mass basis far more efficiently than a center can.

The question as to the general level of conferences offered at a university-based center is influenced by whether its staff regards it as a single-function or a multiple-function agency. If it is devoted solely to teaching, the only way by which it can achieve a distinguished status is by focusing on university conferences, as defined by the institution concerned. If training and research are also accepted as functions, it is essential to have a range of levels enabling the students in training to have greater experience than otherwise,' and insuring that the research undertaken is not restricted to the study of a narrowly circumscribed population. Nobody criticizes the laboratory school for teaching elementary subjects if it does so as a means of training teachers or conducting research. The university hospital must likewise be concerned with common and simple diseases in order to familiarize future doctors with them and to facilitate research into their causes and cures.

2. The educational purpose of a center should be related to the unique nature of its university. Every university has a collectively-shared image of itself and its functions. The distinctiveness in the ethos of institutions may be suggested by calling roll of some of those which have developed centers for residential continuing education: Michigan State University, the University

49

of Maryland, The University of Chicago, the Virginia Polytechnic Institute, the University of Oklahoma, Notre Dame, Oxford, and Columbia. How different they are from one another and how ridiculous it would be if they sought uniformity in the patterning of their conferences ! Since a university has many facets, its program of residential continuing education should be highly complex but it should also have coherent principles of operation and a unity of theme and approach which both reflects and extends the distinctive conception that the institution has of itself.

3. Conferences should be long enough and sufficiently well designed for the maximum possible educational impact. Almost two-thirds of the conferences held at ten American universities in 1966 lasted three days or less; many were only a day in duration. Such brief meetings, particularly if there is no preceding preparation by participants and no follow-up, may have little educative effect. To achieve objectives of a worthwhile sort, at least three kinds of development should take place. First, many conferences ought to be longer than they are. Second, preparatory and sequential educational activities need to be devised. Third, and most important, conferences must be skillfully planned to take every advantage of the time available. With increasing experience and the use of the results of research on residential continuing education, universities can learn to make the conference one of the most effective forms of education they offer.

A center which accepts teaching as its sole function will almost automatical have a variety of conference types, being led to do so by the complexity of specific objectives served. A triple-function center must, however, make certain that it uses most or all of the program types suggested by the Buskey taxonomy so that well-rounded experience can be offered to the adult educators being trained and insuring that the necessary variety of research material is available.

4. The program of residential continuing education should be fully accepted as an essential responsibility of the university. Boards of trustees,

50

administrators, and faculty members must be both firm and creative in accepting such responsibility. Because of the pressures of academic life, a relatively few university authorities may have sustained contact with residential continuing education, but most of them should work with it at least occasionally and view it as an integral part of their work. While the application of the other principles in the present list will help in this respect, the staff of the center must find ways to strengthen general underatanding of its work as it discharges its three purposes. In a later section of this essay, methods will be suggested for achieving this end.

One important symbol of the full acceptance of the center as an integral part of the university is that it has the same rights to the university's funds and the same fiscal opportunities as do other educational units. Among such rights and opportunities are: freedom from the need to balance the budget from the center's earnings each year; freedom from the need to pay off capital expenditures out of current income; adequate funds for research, staff training, and experimentation with new programming; the right to use accumulated reserves; the right of access to outside donors or grantors; and the assistance of the university's development and information staff in helping the center secure financing and good public relations.

5. <u>Programs of residential continuing education should be guided by men and women of stature and competence.</u> They should be skilled in designing and conducting many different kinds of conferences, and they should be able to speak as university staff members with ideas and convictions about the importance of continuing education. A later section of this essay will return to this theme.

6. <u>Programs of continuing education should make important intellectual contributions to the university.</u> A university profits by having as participants in its programs men and women of intellectual capacity who can apply balanced and practical judgment to the occasionally angular viewpoints of specialists. The ideas of the outside world are brought to the center in

a steady stream and can give rise to new approaches to teaching and research if the faculty will only heed them. Also, if the university does its work well, it sends back into the community men and women with a deeper appreciation of the value of scholarship and with a desire to support and defend them.

The Training Function

The center for residential continuing education is related to the emerging field of adult education in much the same way that the teaching hospital is related to the health professions and the laboratory school is related to elementary and secondary school teaching. Each institutional type tries in formalized ways to have a part in the pre-service and in-service training of those who embark on careers in the occupations relevant to its work. Since the center's offering is related to the whole range of a university's knowledge and its method is applicable to many fields of scholarship, it performs additional important but less clear-cut training functions. These overlap with both the teaching and the research functions, but that very overlapping indicates how essential it is to maintain the center's multipurpose orientation.

An Adjunct to Graduate Study in Adult Education: The most sustained use of a center in training educators of adults occurs when it becomes the site of a special internship. Just as a medical or nursing student gains clinical experience in a hospital and a prospective teacher undertakes observation and practice in a laboratory school, some of the students in doctoral or master's programs in adult education incorporate supervised work in a center into their graduate study. At several universities - including Chicago, Michigan State, and Nebraska - internships have been provided to enable such students to work for varying lengths of time in the center, learning every aspect of its operation, with particular reference to its methods of conceiving, designing, and conducting conferences. These interns receive two kinds of supervision: from the staff of the center in terms of the performance of duties; and from a graduate professor in terms of the application of theoretical understanding.

52

A less intensive experience than the internship is also made available on some campuses to all graduate students in adult education. This experience comes from courses, guided work experience, participation, observation, the reading of research reports, and close association with interns. Ordinarily, the entire student group in adult education becomes familiar with the promise and the problems of the center. Some students use it as a place to collect data for their papers and theses. The future careers of most graduate students in adult education will involve them to some degree in the sponsorship or administration of conferences. The experience gained in the center should give them insights and skills to help them in their future practice.

An Adjunct to Professional Study in Other Fields: A few universities teach hotel and restaurant administration and at least one of them, Michigan State University, uses its center for residential continuing education as a place for study and work experience, much as university programs in hospital administration use the teaching hospital for the same purpose. More generally, the conferences sponsored by various university departments often involve some service by their graduate students. While this exposure is far from being systematic training, it does provide a substantial number of students with some insight into the operation of a center and the principles of program design.

A Means of Continuing Education for Educators of Adults: People who are making a career out of the education of adults are no more exempt from the need for continuing education than are the members of any other profession. The university centers (particularly when they are on campuses with strong graduate departments of adult education) offer an important means for understanding this purpose. Some institutions - among them Chicago, Michigan State, Syracuse, and Wisconsin - have conducted annual conferences or workshops for persons concerned with higher adult education, librarianship, community college service, or other specialized fields of work. Oxford has sponsored a number of special conferences, particularly ones which draw an international clientele. Other universities provide more sporadic services, but in the aggregate the work done is substantial.

The Training of Practitioners: The term "practitioner" is here used to signify that very large and amorphous group of people who carry forward most of the work of adult education. Usually they have been untrained in any formal sense for such duties; they came into service, they say, "by the back door." Some are paid; others are volunteers. Some teach; others guide, direct, and counsel; still others do organizational work. Some are full-time; some are part-time. They serve in many agencies, great and small: public evening schools, libraries, churches, industry, unions, voluntary associations, settlement houses, government projects, proprietary schools, and many others. For this large group of people, university centers of continuing education have provided a wide range of residential learning experiences.

Between 1953 and 1965, for example, Indiana University conducted more than 150 institutes on adult education involving more than 4,000 trainees from 50 states and 15 foreign countries. Each institute "usually extends for 5 1/2 days and is conducted at a residential center. About thirty trainees and five staff members take part. The trainee spends considerable time in small group laboratory and practice sessions. Theory is presented in general sessions, and careful study of materials is encouraged. Upon completion of the experience, the trainee receives a certificate of recognition from the University. Under certain conditions, graduate credit in adult education can be earned, and about 10 percent of the trainees obtain credit."[1] While few other universities – perhaps none – would be able to equal Indiana's continuing record, most university residential continuing education programs can cite some conferences designed to assist practitioners of adult education.

These conferences are of four kinds. Some are designed around institutional needs. They may be planned specifically for such persons as librarians, training directors in industry, public school adult educators, church workers, or representatives of voluntary associations, such as the

_____

[1] Robert M. Smith; "One Hundred and Fifty Institutes in Adult Education," Adult Leadership, XIV (September, 1965), pp. 90-91.

P. T. A. Others are organized to meet the needs of some program of service.
In recent years, for example, many universities (often in conjunction with
other agencies) have supported conferences designed to assist literacy
teachers. Still other conferences aim to convey some skill or body of knowledge required by educators of adults, as in the creativity or sensitivity
training conferences now held at many universities. Finally, generalized
opportunities for learning about adult education are offered, regularly or
sporadically, at a number of higher educational institutions. Colorado, for
example, has offered adult education workshops in   collaboration with the
State Department of Education. A number of universities have sponsored
and financed the meetings of adult educational associations.

The Creation of New Ideas and Syntheses: One of the most important
training functions of a university center for residential continuing education is
to bring together academic leaders of adult education and their non-campus
colleagues to explore various problems with the general hope of bringing
about a sounder knowledge base for the field. A number of the papers presented at annual Michigan State conferences have been published, as has the
report of a national conference on adult literacy teaching, held at Chicago.
Almost every year, Syracuse University sponsors a high-level assembly
of educators of adults and invited specialists in other fields to present papers
and discuss some aspect of adult learning. Among the topics dealt with have
been the sociological, psychological, and anthropological backgrounds of adult
education, and the dynamics of change in universities.

The In-service Education of the University's Staff: The provision
of adult education is now an important activity of most American universities.
Many feel the need continuously to educate their own faculty members and
administrators for adequate task performance. In a later section of this
essay, attention will be devoted to the in-service education of the people who
work in the center itself, but here the importance of reaching two other
audiences will be noted.

The members of the university extension staff who are not concerned with the operation of the center for residential continuing education can often use it for their own in-service training. Such people may be widely dispersed geographically and it is therefore particularly important to provide them a common educational experience by bringing them together into a residential situation. In most states, the Cooperative Extension Service holds annual extension conferences as well as special meetings devoted to particular topics. In those states in which Cooperative and general extension activities have been merged, periodic conferences provide a means for helping two or more groups of staff members to come to know one another and to study the matters with which they have a common concern.

Some universities have tried to encourage responsiveness to continuing education on the part of faculty members by offering special conferences in which a sense of freshness and novelty as well as an atmosphere of concentration is achieved by a residential program at some place other than the campus, often a rural retreat. Thus Syracuse University for some years had invitational conferences for the faculty of its evening college; at these meetings, held in a university-maintained center in the Adirondacks, faculty members could meet, discuss their problems, and hear presentations in a relaxed and congenial setting. Oklahoma and Michigan State have used the same principle, taking scholars and administrators to a residential conference at which they could learn about present extension activities and shape plans for new programs especially designed for adults.

A Means of Acquainting the Future Leaders of Society and the Academic World with the Significance of Conferences: Every center can help shape the future climate of opinion for itself and its parallel centers on other campuses by trying to reach as many university students as possible with the ideas and practices of continuing education. Meaningful ways of effecting this relationship in an intensive fashion have already been mentioned, but the staffs of centers might well ponder whether they could discharge this "training" function in other ways as well. Some of the students will become the academic, professional, and political leaders of the future. Involvement in the activities of the center will help them to understand and possibly to support its work. As yet these efforts at involvement have been largely sporadic and accidental, but no apparent reason exists for not making them more continuous and substantial.

The Research Function

The most obvious, clear-cut, and widespread use of centers for residential education to advance research comes as a by-product of the teaching or training functions when they sponsor, help to design, and administer conferences which bring together research workers, including faculty members, outside specialists, or both. Virtually every university center for continuing education houses such conferences each year, and their content ranges widely across the whole spectrum of knowledge. The sponsorship of such conferences is highly important to a center in discharging its basic functions and in bringing it closer to the heart of the faculty's concerns and interests, particularly if the staff of the center has been able to provide creative and effective program-planning and administrative assistance.

But as has been demonstrated by studies summarized earlier, a center for residential continuing education can itself be the focus of research and its processes subjected to objective analysis. The sponsorship of such investigations is not as yet a major activity of such centers, but they are doing enough in this respect to make it clear that this function is an actual rather than a potential one. It is carried out at several levels of abstraction, which will here be described and illustrated.

Improvement-of-service Studies: Special studies to improve the conference program are undertaken by virtually every university center, sometimes on a continuing basis, sometimes only fitfully. At Nebraska, for example, an effort has been made to build objective evaluation into every conference, and the results of the measurement of progress are used to improve subsequent performance. At Colorado, a systematic investigation was made of the publics whom the university was serving in order to guide future programming. Sometimes improvement-of-service studies are carried out with rigor and on a long-range basis. At Oklahoma, for example, the American Journal of Nursing gave funds to support a refresher course for nurses who had been out of practice but wished to rejoin the profession. The grant provided for an evaluation at the end of the program, two years later, and five years later. Improvement-of-service studies are normal parts of an ongoing program and are not designed to yield general principles, to test models, or to carry out other major research functions. At their best, however, they provide examples of innovative practice which may stimulate other centers to do likewise or furnish information which can be put to use.

Basic Data Collection: As yet, most university centers collect only such information about performance as overworked administrators can find time to record, and each center has its own categories for analyzing this information. There are no general indices of performance such as are common in other forms of institutional administration. Therefore, the directors of centers and those to whom they report can often do little to describe their operations objectively or to compare them with those of other universities. The net result was expressed by a British observer:

> . . . a great deal of material is going dead. When I say 'dead'
> I mean it is not going anywhere. Most of us who have to do with
> running conferences do quite faithfully keep an observation
> record of a descriptive type, and alongside the work we do for
> . . . ourselves we are often asked to produce something called
> a report . . . I think there is a great deal of valuable material
> being lost because we feel it is not systematized enough to hand to anybody. [1]

In an effort to try to change this situation, a group of universities (ranging in number from eleven to fourteen) collaborated from 1962 to 1968 in developing, testing, and using a common reporting form. Each conference was described by its co-ordinator in terms of its content, level, planning, and follow-up procedures, kinds of activities, nature of participants involved, and other matters. All such reports were sent to a central source, and

---

[1]Gwendolyn Chesters, in Capes, Communication or Conflict, p. 164.

analyzed to provide periodic summations of performance by each center. As a result, it became possible for the first time for each university to have a clear picture of the pattern of operation of its own center and to compare it with those of other universities.[1]

Studies of Conference Procedures and Processes: As has been illustrated earlier by the studies of Buskey, Florell, Jackson, Lacognata, Stevenson, Welden, Kafka, and Fales, the conference itself or the center which administers it can be used as bases for complex and well-designed research. Other similar studies will be noted later. Probably the great bulk of investigation at the university-based centers will be of this sort.

The Testing of General Hypotheses in the Social Sciences: Centers also lend themselves to studies of a more general nature. A program of residential continuing education creates new social patterns and frameworks, different ways to approach problems, and direct contacts among men and women from diverse backgrounds. In the course of a year, a great range of people drawn from the community comes to such programs, and research workers in the university or elsewhere who are interested in studying the individual, the group, or various patterns of human association will find opportunities for doing so in a center.

One unusually promising field for investigation is the nature of the group process. At the University of Wisconsin Robert Boyd is conducting a series of studies of the interaction of individuals in the discussion process. To facilitate this research, an observation booth with one-way glass has been set up adjacent to a conference room. Paul Byers has presented a fascinating pictorial record of the interactive changes which occur in the conference setting.[2] Herbert Thelen of the University of Chicago is interested in the way the productivity of a group is influenced by the kinds of people who compose it. It is a common observation that some small groups, because of

---

[1] This entire collaboration was sponsored by the Studies and Training Program in Continuing Education and is described by Lawrence E. Devlin and Ann Litchfield in Continuing Education Reports Numbers Fifteen and Sixteen, The University of Chicago, 1967.

[2] Mead and Byers, The Small Conference.

59

their members' inability to work together, end their meetings with no clear outcomes and with feelings of disappointment and frustration. Other small groups, however, seem to be productive of good results and considerable satisfaction. Thelen investigated this question by analyzing the personality traits of conference-goers, and then grouped them in various ways to discover which combinations led to the greatest productivity.[1]

In another study, Howard Sulkin examined the differential impact of teaching methods on adults. At a number of five-day management-training conferences, he used a battery of instruments to identify the personality type of each participant according to a classification scheme developed by Eysenck. The training patterns were then controlled so that the same body of content was taught in two different ways: by lecture and by case-discussion. Increase in cognitive knowledge was then assessed using a variety of measures. Sulkin found that the Eysenck categories of personality did not seem to be significantly related to the response of students to the two educational techniques.[2]

In still another study, Sherman Sheffield used conference attenders as informants on the extent and nature of their own continuing education. He administered a lengthy instrument of his own devising to 453 adults attending twenty educational conferences of various sorts at eight American universities. The results showed that the educational participation of adults can be measured on a scale whose scores are distributed in a normal curve, and that five clear-cut orientation patterns to education can be found among adults: those who seek learning for its own sake, those who use it to achieve personal goals, those who use it to achieve social goals, those who enjoy the process of learning, and those who find

---

[1]Herbert Thelen, Role Perception and Task Performance of Experimentally Composed Small Groups, Report #1 from N. I. M. H. Project "Use of Small Groups to Adapt Problem Students," 1965-1970.

[2]Howard Sulkin, "Relationship between Participant Personality and Teaching Methods in Management Training" (unpublished doctoral dissertation, The University of Chicago, 1969).

in it a form of escape. While Sheffield was primarily concerned with in dividual learners, he was able to draw some important implications for the operation of the centers themselves. For example, he noted that

in each individual conference with a representative attendance
of sixteen or more learners, all five orientations are represented.
Here again the educator must recognize the different orientations
as being represented in the conferees and he must take some
steps to accommodate these motivations for maximum educational
effect.[1]

The Testing of Theoretical Models: Such studies as the foregoing are still too few in number to have established lines or traditions of research, and most investigations have been too severely limited in character to provide definitive answers to the questions raised in them. But it is not too much to hope that sustained research in university-based centers might sometime be used for the testing of theoretical models in education, social psychology, or other fields of investigation. One promising prospect, for example, was suggested ty A. T. M. Wilson of the Tavistock Institute in London:

What are the special characteristics of conferences which
make them unusual as social institutions? One characteristic
which makes them different is that they are, for example,
short-duration meetings of people, and this presents a whole
variety of problems- of moving from one situation, of setting
up temporary role-relationships with other conference members,
and then moving back again . . . From the point of view of
the research worker opportunities which are more than an hour
in duration, especially a conference of five days, are rich in
research possibilities. I have had one general experience which
supports this view...the study of temporary communities designed
to assist returning prisoners of war. Men passed through on
a five-week basis, coming from one country to another, and
the experience of these transitional communities was, technically,
by far the richest of all the rich military experiences we had.
It presented tremendous opportunities for studying the process
of de-socialization, re-socialization, interplay of personality
and structure, modification of values, and the re-development
of social skills; a wide range of things was illustrated. The
same type of process, in less obvious form, lies hidden in the

---

[1]Sherman Sheffield, "The Orientations of Adult Continuing Learners" (unpublished doctoral dissertation, The University of Chicago, 1962), p. 146.

golden hills of conference research of almost any kind.[1]

As this passage suggests, the study of conferences might be used to illustrate or to test what Merton has called a "theory of the middle range," which goes beyond specific inquiries to deal with a larger framework of explanation. A social synthesis of this sort has been provided by Matthew Miles in a paper, "On Temporary Systems." Miles highlights the relevance of conferences to his thought by naming them first in the lengthy list of "interstitial, temporary structures" which "operate both within permanant organizations and between them," and whose "members hold from the start the basic assumption that - at some more or less clearly defined point in time - they will cease to be."[2] Miles omits from his investigation all unplanned events "such as political crises, mobs, panics, and physical disasters . . since the onset of such systems is usually adventitious, and terminal times usually remain vague. This implies that the notion of willedness is important in considering temporary systems." (p. 439)

Miles' analysis of such systems moves through several phases. He first examines the time duration of systems, suggesting that they can be classified as to whether their proposed ending is fixed chronologically, related to the happening of an external event, or linked to the achievement of some result. (p. 441) He goes on to discuss the functions of temporary systems. Then comes the major part of the paper, a detailed accounting of all the characteristics of temporary systems, divided up among those which are " 'input' characteristics appearing at the time of designing or setting up the temporary system;" 'process' characteristics occurring during the life of the system; and 'output' characteristics - the resultant changes in persons, groups and organizations." (p. 452) He then investigates some of the problems and dysfunctions of temporary systems, such as unrealistic goal-setting, lack of process skills, and alienation. (pp. 480- 82) Finally , he deals with the

---

[1]In Communication or Conflict, pp. 170-171.

[2]Matthew Miles, "On Temporary Systems, " in Innovations in Education, edited by Matthew Miles (New York: Columbia University Press, 1966) , pp. 437-38. Other quotations from this work will be located by putting page numbers in parentheses in the text.

importance of temporary systems for educational innovation and concludes
with these words: "Until we genuinely understand that 'the only constant is
change,' it will be hard for us to realize that our engagement with the stress,
adventure, and creative struggle of one temporary system after another is
indeed 'the way we live now.'" (p. 486)

At every point in this long and complex analysis, the specialist in
residential continuing education is tempted to apply Miles' formulations,
particularly since it is clear that while the author has a far broader frame
of reference than the learning conference, it is at all points central to his
thought. Research workers may use this framework as a source for hypotheses; the earlier-mentioned study by Kafka has already done so. Practical
men may use it to understand somewhat better than before their own ways of
work and, as a result of that understanding, to improve their performance.
Both may be able to speak with greater authority and conviction than before on
those elements which lie beneath the surface of residential continuing educa-
cation and determine its ultimate worth and meaning.

Toward a General Theory : Such models as the one proposed by Miles
may some day lead to even broader theoretical analyses. Pestalozzi,
Froebel, Montessori, Dewey, and Piaget used controlled observation in
schools and playgrounds to develop theories of child growth and education.
Freud, Jung, Adler, and other psychoanalysts built general conceptions of
personality based upon treatment of the mentally ill. Rogers and other psychol-
ogists were able to transfer their experience in counseling and testing centers
to define and describe the helping relationship of one individual to another.
It is possible that some day a center for residential continuing education will
serve as the instrument which enables an investigator or a philosopher to
develop and test a fundamental theory of human behavior.

The Staffing of the Center Program

The three functions of the university-based center for residential
continuing education are so challenging that they lay a heavy burden on the
program staff, and the rapid growth of centers has made it difficult to find

enough people to discharge these exacting tasks. Some positions have been occupied by creative pioneers, imbued with a sense of mission and eager to invent and establish the ways by which that mission could be fulfilled. For the most part, however, jobs have been occupied by men and women chosen for their general capacities of intellect, personality, and background, but who realize that they must learn on the job many of the things they should know. This learning has chiefly come from apprenticeship, trial-and-error, sporadic theorizing, the use of principles borrowed from other forms of education, and the development of a few rough-and-ready rules of thumb derived from practical experience.

The Pattern of Program Staffing: Most centers have now established a tri-level pattern of program staffing. (The supporting staff will be described later.) The central position is that of the conference coordinator, who designs and helps to design a conference, makes the necessary personal and material arrangements for it, oversees and helps in its actual operation, and reports on its accomplishments. The program director occasionally serves as a conference coordinator, but he also administers the work of the other people engaged in these tasks. In many cases, he serves as director of the center itself, thus overseeing its entire physical and educational operation. The aide (sometimes called an assistant coordinator or some other title) is a junior staff member, engaged to facilitate the operation in any way he can. He may be learning to be a coordinator, but at the time of his service he has no established professional standing. He performs whatever tasks are needed. Some centers do not have aides, and, in such cases, the coordinators - and sometimes even the program director - must carry out the facilitative tasks required. In addition to the three major kinds of staff members, a center may have other kinds of program positions, such as people on joint appointment with academic departments or other extension units, or evening and week-end "duty officers."

The Degree of Professionalism of the Program Staff: The question has been frequently and insistently raised as to whether a separate occupational category based on conference programming should be developed. There are four general responses to this question, though it is impossible to estimate how widely each is believed: (1) There should be no occupational differentiation at all; the university should simply find talented people and give them the task of conference leadership. (2) The staff members of a university extension division should make up a generalized group, some of whom work in conferences, some at other tasks. This group should be drawn from many sources, but should be essentially chosen on grounds of native or acquired ability. Its members do not need special training in adult education. (3) There should be a special occupational group of career workers in conference leadership (as there are in some European countries), selected by various means but dedicated to the task of doing its special job supremely well and therefore constantly studying, how to improve. (4) Conference coordinators and administrators should make up one of the many categories of positions in the broad field of adult education. To do their work well such people require a great deal of specialized knowledge and competence about residential continuing education. Beyond the specifics, however, lies generalized knowledge which can be most efficiently conveyed through formal study, both prior to service and during it.

Program staff members may acquire their expertise in many ways, but its essential nature can be broadly outlined. They must be able to identify a possible educational activity, judge its feasibility, refine its objectives, design its format, fit it into any larger patterns of activity which influence its success, conduct it, measure its results, and appraise its accomplishments. In designing the format, they must select human and physical resources, identify (and sometimes train) leaders, choose the methods to be used, organize a schedule which provides a proper sequence of activities, develop ways to create social reinforcement among participants, and consider how the various roles and relationships of the people concerned are to be established and made operative. So far as is possible in a group activity, they should measure the educative impact on each individual who attends,

identify the criteria of evaluation, and make the conference design clear
to everyone concerned. Each separate conference must be fitted into the
overall program of the center, of the university, and of the outside
associations which may serve as co-sponsors; it must be financed; it
must be interpreted to any publics related to it; and sometimes guidance
must be given to the participants either at the time they decide to come to the
conference or later.

In a minimal kind of way, these tasks can be performed mechanically
and learned as a craft through routine experience. Most centers have
developed some kind of program planning checklist, based on the successes
and failures of the past, and it can be used in a rote fashion to be sure that
nothing important is forgotten.[1] In any such usage, the coordinator puts
together the predetermined pieces of a conference, leaving any substantial
decisions as to form or content to other people. During the actual operation,
he does whatever he can to ease and support its progress. After it is over,
he tidies up loose ends. Such a pattern of operation is all too common.
In a 1964 study of several centers, Chester Leathers and William Griffith
reached the severe conclusion that:

> The prevailing assumption seems to be that coordinators are simply
> facilitatorsor administrators who are not expected to possess any
> educational expertise, express an opinion on the conference program,
> or have any voice in shaping the learning experience. Loaded down
> with administrative details of conferences planned by others who
> may have little appreciation of the knowledge and skills required
> to develop effective conferences, coordinators seldom have the
> opportunity to perform the role of educator. Because present per-
> formance is all too often viewed as the precedent for the future,
> the possibility of coordinators' developing an image as educators is
> scant.[2]

But the interrelated body of tasks which collectively make up the
experience of conference coordinators can also become the focus of an

---

[1] For an example of such a check-list, see: Frank C. Goodell, "A Program Planning Checklist for the Meeting Planner," Adult Leadership,
XVIII (December, 1969), pp. 180-181.

[2] Chester W. Leathers and William S. Griffith, "The Conference Coordinator: Educator or Facilitator?" Continuing Education Report Number
Two, The University of Chicago, 1965.

emerging profession. Each such task is capable of exhaustive theoretical analysis and a vast body of research. For example, the social reinforcement of learning has been the subject of an enormous literature in social psychology and education; the coordinator who wants to know more about the subject will never come to the end of the resources available to him. He can also make his own contribution to the knowledge base which supports his expertise. To cite but one example, Ross Waller has outlined the methods developed and used for this purpose at Holly Royde, the center at Manchester University in England.[1]

The desire to achieve the status of a professional rather than a routine craftsman has been a continuing aspiration of coordinators. Leathers and Griffith found that their respondents ranked their actual roles in order as: (1) administrator, (2) facilitator, and (3) educator. By contrast, their ideal order of roles was: (1) educator, (2) administrator, and (3) facilitator. The frustrations inherent in this reversal of roles has caused many coordinators to learn conference work. On the other hand, the desire to achieve a reordering in practice has led some program staffs to establish new priorities and has motivated more than a few coordinators to prepare themselves to be professionals by advanced graduate study in adult education and allied fields.

Much of the in-service education provided to program staff members has been informal. It occurs as a director guides and supervises a coordinator or aides in the performance of his work, and as others on the staff gradually acculturate the new member in both standards and performmance skills. Some centers, however, have initiated and maintained a formal program of continuous staff training. At the Georgia Center for Continuing Education, for example, the staff meets regularly for this purpose. One of its activities is the analysis of cases, in which each coordinator in turn leads a discussion on the planning process of a conference for which he has been responsible. The group attempts to reconstruct its program development and execution, step by step. As a change of pace, a

---

[1]Ross D. Waller, Methods at Holly Royde (London: National Institute of Adult Education, 1965).

67

Center staff member from another department (such as food service, the library, or the registration desk) is occasionally invited to discuss that department's function in the overall operation of the Center. The staff also periodically schedules a series of breakfast discussion meetings at which it works its way through a coordinated course, such as Great Decisions or Basic Issues of Man. Such staff meetings give the group a common body of ideas and processes, reinforced by the continuing relationships among the director, the coordinators, and the aides.

The Program Director: The program director is the focal educational figure of the center. Ideally, he should understand and be able to apply the expertise required of the coordinators and aides, he should be an effective supervisor of their work, and he should be able to collaborate constructively with the people whose responsibilities relate directly to his own: the other university administrators, the faculty, and the individuals and groups outside the university who influence its conference programming. In doing so, he must try to fulfill the three functions of the center, he must provide educational and executive leadership to his staff, and he must accept responsibility for the myriad activities required of the operation of a highly complex program.

His overall conception of his task has an important influence on the selection and operation of conferences. Donald Deppe, using a number of social psychological concepts, has envisioned the program director as operating at the boundary of the university. [1] He is, in a sense, marginal to its traditional central purposes and, in fact, the literature of conference leadership is filled with discussions of "marginality," the term usually being used in a negative or critical sense. But to Deppe, the director is a boundary-definer, one who uses his judgments and values to decide what shall or shall not be admitted into the university's programs and, if it is admitted, on what terms. He sees constant opportunities for service and he also

---

[1] The present summary of this study is taken from: Donald A. Deppe, "The Conference Director as a Boundary Definer of the University" (unpublished doctoral dissertation, The University of Chicago, 1965). Much of the material used is also contained in: Donald A. Deppe, "The Adult Educator: Marginal Man and Boundary Definer," Adult Leadership, XVIII (October, 1969), pp. 119-20, 129-30.

feels pressure from various sources. Opportunity and pressure may originate from within the institution or outside it. Although his specific actions vary as he responds to particular situations, the director has a hierarchy of values and a behavioral predisposition which determine his general stance. Using these conceptions, Deppe hypothesized that program directors could be classified into dominant role types in terms of their usual response to the boundary-defining role.

In reviewing the data he collected on forty-five program directors, however, Deppe was struck by the fact that, at a deeper level of analysis which viewed each man as a total individual and not solely as a boundary definer, five composite portraits tended to emerge.[1] Thirty-nine subjects could be classified as fitting one of these basic orientations. The client-oriented program director (of whom Deppe found eight cases) is one whose major concern is for the well-being of the persons who participate in the various programs administered by the conference division. The operations-oriented director (nine cases) is one who is interested primarily in "producing a good show," not so much in terms of dramatic movement or esthetic coherence, as in terms of efficient management. The image-oriented director (four cases) has as his chief concern the projection of a favorable conception of the university to those who participate in the programs of continuing education. The institution-oriented director (ten cases) is not nearly as much interested in projecting an image of the university as he is in discovering and understanding its purposes and traditions. He then seeks to make his role conform to his understanding of these institutional characteristics. The problem-oriented director (eight cases) sees problems in society that cry out for solution, and his first concern is to try to mobilize whatever educational resources he can muster toward the solution of those problems.

These five types of program directors are charged with responsibilities having implications of which they are sometimes only faintly aware,

---

[1] These five orientations have been further studied in: David S. Coleman, "A Study of the Leader Behavior of the Selected Directors of University Conference Operations" (unpublished doctoral dissertation, The University of Wisconsin, 1969).

but as surely as these individuals exist, they are helping to shape their universities. Certain gross consequences appear, for example, when one looks at the pronounced differences between the client-oriented director and the institution-oriented director. A program shaped by the former, in a situation which gives him some degree of autonomy, will probably result in a highly flexible boundary that shifts with little resistance to the pressures of demands for service. A program shaped by the latter, if he is likewise free to exercise his dominant predisposition, will produce a less flexible boundary, which in turn may tend to insulate the institution from external pressures. In one instance the relationships between the university and its environment are largely determined from without; in the other case these relationships are established from within.

The Supporting Staff and Functions[1]

A residential center is a campus in miniature, with all of the problems generally associated with an institution's facilities. People sleep in it, eat in it, meet in it, play in it, park in it, walk on the grass, and do office work. The center manager (who may or may not also be the program director) regulates traffic, keeps efficient personnel on the job, corrects mechanical and structural breakdowns, refurbishes and renews worn furnishings and decor, reallocates space for new or revised uses, plans future expansions, argues with suppliers, and keeps expenses near income. He has problems with the kitchen, vending machines, first-aid and medical services, crabgrass and Dutch elm disease, inflation, inventories, union contracts, minimum wages, security from within and without, taxis, buses, and records; with

---

[1]This section is based in large part on an informal memorandum prepared by Thurman White, Vice President of the University of Oklahoma, for the Program of Studies and Training in Continuing Education and is used with his permission. The memorandum itself was published under the title "Financing Residential Centers for Continuing Education" in NUEA Spectator, April-May, 1971.

reports by the day, the week, the month, and the year; with insurance and liability, bonds, bailers, and fire; and with non-registered blondes and other people whose interests are not central to that of the university. He lives with the special equipment; with administrators who direct that a favorite group be given a booking priority over previous commitments; with cancellations of guaranteed and all-but-sure programs; with changes without notice in utility contracts; with extremely low use on weekends and in certain months; and with an almost total risk in raising the money to pay the bills while working inside the rigid control of institutional policies designed for non-adult students.

Among the continuing or occasional staff members a center requires are: (1) those who aid instruction, such as librarians, audio-visual materials specialists, editors, and brochure writers; (2) those who provide hotel accommodation, such as a facilities manager, housekeepers, maids, stock clerks, room clerks, porters, engineers, maintainance men, security guards, newsstand operators, telephone operators, housemen, laundrymen, cashiers, electricians, carpenters, painters, gardeners, window washers, and plumbers; (3) those who provide food and beverage service, such as dietitians, chefs, maitres d'hotel, waiters, busboys, dishwashers, bartenders, cashiers; and (4) those who provide support for the executive processes, such as secretaries, typists, reservation clerks, registration clerks, and accountants. Every person employed in a center has a part - and sometimes a vital part - in the creation of the learning environment it can provide.

A center's total budget must include not merely the allocations required to employ these people or hire the service performed, but also a multitude of other items. Among them are: insurance, staff benefits, replacement of equipment and supplies, redecoration, printing, stationery, employees' meals, flowers and decorations, food and beverages, license fees, newsstand supplies, parking lot supervision, garbage removal, advertising and promotion expense, auditor's fees, legal fees, association dues, trade publications, travel, money collection and delivery, telephones, telegrams, and bad debts.

There are, as well, the inevitable emergencies which always require immediate attention and often involve expenditures; among them are fire, storms, vandalism, theft, power failures, strikes, illness, and death. In some centers continuing provision must also be made for retiring a mortgage, for general university overhead, and for debt service.

This recital of duties and expenses indicates that a university should not undertake lightly the operation of a center, nor should its director assume his role without realizing how much specialized expertise he will need to perform or to supervise. A small center may have a director-of-all-work who does everything himself. A large center can hire the services performed and may even be able to provide several levels of specialized supervision. Ultimately, however, like the manager of any other major educational program, the center director must accept final responsibility for everything.

These burdens bear down hardest on the man who first assumes the direction of a center. He must build everything up from the beginning: guiding the designing and construction of a new building or the alteration of an existing one; engaging and training both the program and supportive staff; and developing a team spirit among its members while encountering all the problems of opening a new institution. While such a task is exciting, it is also wearing. It is therefore not surprising that the belief has grown up in university circles that the first director of a center for continuing education is expendable; soon after the building enters into service, his tenure ends, either by his own choice or by that of the university. Fortunately, as institutions have learned to plan more carefully than before, this bit of folklore is being belied by experience.

The term "center director" has been used in foregoing pages as though all such institutions had one guiding administrator. Such is not necessarily the case. Some university centers (such as Arden House of Columbia) are operated solely as physical facilities, with programs designed and conducted by anyone who contracts for their services. Even when a university maintains a center as a purely educational institution under its own control, program supervision may follow one channel of authority up to the president, and the administration of building operations may follow another. Such a division can be made to work only if there is close supervision at every level on institutional policy, if rules and regulations are carefully established but with agreements as to who may waive them in emergencies, and if the various staff members develop a capacity to work easily and flexibly with one another. Even when these conditions prevail, occasional catastrophes can occur. For example, a program staff may feel that a conference in progress can be saved only by a relaxation of some food-service regulation which has become a point at issue among the conferees; the building manager may feel that to do so would set a bad precedent; and before higher authorities can be reached and brought into agreement, the conference may fail, the relationships among staff members become strained and perhaps broken, with irreparable loss to the reputation of the center and its university.

Finance

The foregoing analysis has indicated the major items of expenditure of a center and has suggested such sources of income as that derived from the renting of hotel rooms and other accommodations, and the use of the restaurant and bar. In both capital costs and continuing operation, however, certain other sources are substantial. They include: foundations; federal, state, and local governments; business and industry; professional and voluntary associations; gifts by individuals; fees paid by conferees; and general institutional support. A hidden resource is the contributed time of faculty and other university staff members as well as of all the many other people who take part in a center's programs who receive little or no remuneration or whose salaries are carried on other budgets. Every center would be much poorer without their services than it now is - and some centers would not be able to survive at all.

Accounting systems and practices vary so much from one university to another that no comparable data for center operation have yet been developed. Sometimes no separate comprehensive budget is kept for the center; income and expenditure are distributed among other university accounts. General

73

university overhead may or may not be charged against a center's costs and, if so, the amount may be determined on any of a number of bases. The decision as to what should or should not be charged against a budget is also variable. The full salary of one extension division   staff member may thus be allocated, though only half his time is spent as a conference coordinator, while another extension staff member who also serves in this capacity to the same extent is paid entirely from other funds. A line item budget may be maintained and may appear to cover all categories of income or costs; yet the director may also have one or more revolving funds with relative freedom to allocate receipts or expenditures among them. One center, for example, showed a remarkable capacity to maintain a "break-even" budget, with an occasional modest annual profit or loss. Yet it also made periodic substantial improvements to its building, finding the resources for them from unexplained accumulations of funds.

It is almost universally expected that centers will balance outgo with income. Sometimes, as suggested above, this relationship is manipulated in order to assure that the financial aim is met. When the general university administrators who oversee accounts feel that a center is not in fact   making its own way, they are likely to impose curbs on the program or on   the building operation. Similarly, if a profit is shown, an expansion of staff and services may be allowed, though there is also a tendency for the "university overhead" account to be increased. An excellent theoretical assertion can be made that the center, since it is essentially educative, should have the same right to general resources as, say, the law school or the department of English. However irrefutable this argument may be in theory, it has not proved to be convincing on very many campuses, particularly in recent hard-pressed years. A university may be willing to absorb deficits for a while, particularly when a center is just getting started, but eventually it is expected to pay its own way and, if it can, to return a profit.

This fiscal policy leads to many ills. Centers tend to serve only people from middle- and upper-income groups, denying residential education to those who cannot afford to pay the high rates charged. The performance of all three functions is geared to potential income, and training and research tend to be forgotten. Short-range gains are given precedence over long-range profits. The program staff is too small to provide adequate educational leadership and is denied the resources it needs for its work. Its salary scale may be too low to retain outstanding individuals. Broadly-based planning is impossible and a feast-or-famine psychology prevails. The problems are particularly acute where creative programming is concerned for, as Sol Tax has pointed out:

> Further development of experimental models in uniquely important conferences is contingent upon the establishment of certain rather than speculative bases for programming. The current practice of funding conferences on an ad hoc basis has tended to discourage faculty participation, has complicated the planning process, has been costly in terms of staff time, and has, at times, caused the abandonment of promising programs. [1]

These dangers are so evident that it might be assumed they would cause alarm, but Arthur Pelton found in a survey of center administrators that many of them "do not, at this time, perceive a need for changing financial conditions. There is little hope for correcting the present financial dilemma until all center administrators realize the need for changing the present financial practices."[2]

The Problem of Identity

While the residential continuing education center is now well-established on the American academic scene, its place and function are still not understood by all those whose collaboration is required to define and achieve its goals. Even where a center has been in existence on a campus for a period of years, some people think of it as an independent instrument of teaching, training, and research, some as a support for the "regular" campus program,

---

[1]Quoted in Alford, Continuing Education in Action, p. 126.

[2]Arthur E. Pelton, "Financing Residential Adult and Continuing Education" (unpublished doctoral thesis, The University Of Nebraska, 1969), p. 181.

and some as a service to the outside community. It may be viewed as a vehicle
for public relations, as a means for money-making or other developmental
purposes, or as a hotel, restaurant, and bar designed for the convenience of
faculty, students, and guests to the university. As Deppe's study showed, even
the program directors, who uniformly emphasized the educational nature of
their activities, held widely different ideas about the proper way to carry them
out.

The causes for this lack of a clear identity for the center as an institutional
form are its relative newness, its complexity, and its intimate involvement
with the life of the university at many points. A center staff cannot independently
perform its three functions and thereby establish its identity as an educative
service. It exists to extend the frontiers of knowledge for the whole university
and therefore its work is interwoven with that of many other people. They will accept
the center as an educational institution only if their own experience leads them to do so

All universities have two major inner control systems, which exert varying
degrees of force from institution to institution. The first and most visible system
consists of the administrative officers who act as a series of decision points
arranged hierarchically. The second, more obscure and amorphous, is the
faculty, which works, sometimes individually, but more often collectively to main
tain those central values which give a community of scholars its distinctive
character. The modern conception of the university took shape in medieval
times and, except for the church, the university is the oldest of man's formal
institutions. This ancient tradition is centered in teaching and research, the
domain of the faculty. The administration and the faculty systems of control
work together fairly well; sometimes one is dominant and sometimes the other,
but ordinarily they have a mutuality of control which, while it must often withstand
strains and factionalism, keeps the university on an even keel.

In the twentieth century, the American University has greatly enlarged
the number of its accepted bodies of content, thus broadening the base of
faculty power but also strengthening the need for administrative coordination.

Equally important, the university has taken on new social responsibilities. The diffusion of agricultural knowledge to farmers, for example, is a world-wide function of government, but the United States is almost unique in locating the administration of this service within the university rather than elsewhere. The growth of departments and of special functions puts a heavy strain on the university's ability to conceptualize or to co-ordinate itself, and has been particularly devisive so far as the two systems are concerned. Paul Miller has put the matter this way:

> Look at any university catalogue, for example, and you
> will find about 50 or 60 of the standard, disciplinary
> departments. Look on through the catalogue and normally
> you will find 150 or more arrangements of offerings
> which do not fit the standard departments. This has
> implications, of course, for areas other than adult
> education. I would argue that administrators have been
> instrumental in bringing about this situation. There are
> two worlds in the university: on the one side is the faculty
> sentiment; and on the other side are the administrators
> who, in order to get support for the university, have had
> to accommodate to the contemporary needs of society. The
> problem is that sometimes we have no one integrating
> the various mechanisms of the institution. [1]

The center for continuing education is one of the important "arrangements of offerings" that administrators have brought into the campus in order to help the university "accommodate to the contemporary needs of society." How has the faculty responded? Tunis Dekker dealt with this question by studying the attitudes which the faculty members participating in conferences at a center had developed toward it. [2] He secured information on an attitude scale from 194 such people at three universities with well-established centers: The University of Georgia,

---

[1] Paul Miller, Excerpts from an Address. Occasional Paper, No. 1. New England Center for Continuing Education, October, 1966.

[2] Tunis Henry Dekker, "Faculty Commitment to University Adult Education" (unpublished doctoral dissertation, The University of Chicago, 1965). Page numbers of various quotations are placed in parentheses after them.

Michigan State University, and Purdue Un iversity.[1] This scale had two sorts
of items selected by Dekker and screened by a panel of judges. One was designed to indicate an <u>integrated</u> orientation, "expressing a sense of coherence
between conference work and the academic duties and professional goals of
the faculty members" (p. 13). Among such items were: to obtain problems
for research and study; to learn more about society outside the university,
and, thereby, improve the courses which I teach; to experiment with the
application of knowledge of practical questions; and to locate materials for
an article (p, 32). The other type of items indicated a <u>segmented</u> orientation, one which expressed a lack of coherence between conference work and
the academic duties and professional goals of the faculty members. Among
such items were: to supplement my income; because membership in a
professional society demanded participation; because it is a departmental
policy; to satisfy a desire to help people irrespective of where I f ind them,
their needs, or their profession (p. 31).

Not surprisingly, Dekker found a significant positive relationship between the frequency and extent of conference participation by a faculty member and the degree to which he expressed the value of integration. The
orientation scores were unrelated to age, academic education, tenure status,
length of appointment in present position, or time allocation to teaching and
research. Academic rank was significant, however. Dekker found that

> Administrators and faculty members in the lower ranks
> exhibited significant tendencies to <u>segmentation,</u> full
> professors exhibited significant tendencies to <u>integration.</u>
> This finding leads to the conclusion that academic per-
> sonnel who have attained the highest possible rank and are
> thus well established within their professions and within
> their institutions find a relevance and value in adult
> education work. (p. 81)

Dekker also used an idea of Kenneth Benne's that the university tends
to be divided into two sectors: the central region (including the faculties
of arts and sciences and the graduate school), and the peripheral region

---

[1] The total number of people who could be identified as having participated for three or more hours in a conference program during the preceding
year was only 285.

(including the professional schools and departments heavily engaged in extension activities). It was hypothesized that faculty members in the central region would have a segmented orientation since they are chiefly interested in traditional forms of content and scholarship, that faculty members in the peripheral region would have an integrated orientation since they are closer than their colleagues to the needs and requirements of organized society and the practicing professionals, and that faculty members with joint appointments would have mixed orientations. These hypotheses proved to be incorrect, for Dekker found that

> Neither differences in the scholarly interests of the central and peripheral regions, nor differences in the way the two regions relate to society can be said to control or limit the orientation of the individual, for no correlation was found between faculty orientation and academic location. (p. 79)

If the observations of Dekker, Miller, and Deppe are accepted as valid, it appears that at each university with a center for residential continuing education, some faculty members (drawn from all parts of the academic community) regard conference participation as an integral part of their work; they seek out the center and are sought by it. Other faculty members participate, but do so for reasons far different from those which motivate their other work. Most faculty members do not participate in the educational program at all and may therefore see the center only as it meets their other casual needs. University administrators may formally define a center as having a predominantly educational function, but they also face problems of institutional maintenance and improvement for which the work of the center provides a ready solution. This reality may keep the center apart from customary university activities. The center staff members fit into this complex system in various ways and influence it by the orientation they hold toward their roles.

Such conclusions lead to speculation about what would happen if a center for continuing education were not added to an existing prestige system but were to be an integral part of a new institution from the beginning. A bold effort to create such a situation was made when Michigan State University guided the development of the University of Nigeria in Nsukka and created a residential continuing education center (financed by a grant from the American government) as one of the first University services. The Center was the focus of campus life for the faculty; it was the point of entry into the University for most visitors and the vantagepoint from which they saw it. Both the literate and illiterate people of the country found it a place of great interest and a source of national pride. Its program offered prestige and advancement to faculty members and administrators, and drew them together within and across disciplines, thus helping to create a sense of intellectual community. The Center related its staff and the institution itself to the educated people of the country, all of whom had been trained elsewhere, and served as the point of origin and maintenance for professional associations and learned societies. In its early years, the Center stood at or near the apex of both faculty and administration prestige systems.[1] What might have happened as time went on, nobody can say, for the Biafran war for independence interrupted the life of the University. It has only recently been reinstituted, with experience too short to predict what role the Center will play in its future.

Pioneers and Perseverers

In the twenty years since major university centers of residential continuing education appeared, they have made progress toward establishing themselves as important new instruments of an old conception of teaching. Center administrators have a better understanding than before of the total enterprise with which they are concerned. Proposals for continuing education centers have a breadth and maturity of conception for greater and more realistic than those put forward earlier. The staffs of the centers are gradually being strengthened; if nothing else, they are acquiring a body of precedent and lore with which to sustain themselves, and they are working with more and more collaborators both inside and outside the university who have become experienced in the conference process. There may be less tendency than before for these staffs to be considered (and to consider themselves) as small groups of

---

[1] A description of the development of the center was provided by Louis A. Doyle in Continuing Education Report Number Ten, The University of Chicago, 1966.

energetic schedule-arrangers or as the proprietors of prosperous and attractive subsidized hotels.

Some progress has also been made in achieving the centers' two other goals: the training of educators of adults and other advanced students; and the conduct of studies and research. As yet, accomplishments in these two respects have been far less substantial than they should have been. Few centers have continuing budgets for these purposes and must sketchily improvise ways of taking care of them on a hit-or-miss basis using the marginal time of staff members, the relatively unskilled and unpaid labor of graduate students undertaking projects and theses, and occasional evaluation funds provided in individual contracts for service.

While progress over the past twenty years cannot be denied, its continuance at the present rate is not likely to bring the centers to their full peak of accomplishment. Vivid and dramatic examples of outstanding achievement are needed. In this paper it has been pointed out again and again that the centers might find useful prototypes in university hospitals and laboratory schools. In both cases, the stature of the institution was established by brilliant leadership. In the case of the teaching hospital, Johns Hopkins led the way in the 1880s when Osler and others created the new conception of extended clinical experience. (In his farewell address to his colleagues in North America, Osler said: "I desire no other epitaph - no hurry about it, I may say - than the statement that I taught medical students in the wards.") Early in the twentieth century, Flexner used the Johns Hopkins example in the report on medical education which changed the whole character of training in that field. In the establishment of the laboratory school, The University of Chicago has provided two dramatic examples. Near the turn of the century, John Dewey combined practice, theory, and the training of teachers so brilliantly that his work has achieved world-wide attention. Twenty years later in the same institution, Henry Morrison developed the mastery concept and the unit method which were to sweep American education. In both periods, the University was educating many of the future leaders of teacher education, who took the idea of the laboratory school with them and put it into practice at other American universities.

But while outstanding leadership in one situation can provide a dramatic and convincing picture of ultimate accomplishment, it cannot establish a national pattern of service. Perseverence is also required. The work of creative pioneers must be imitated and adapted in innumerable situations, each different from the others and each with its own complexities. If the daring pioneer does not emerge, progress can be achieved only by a process of gradual advance in many places. The university center for residential continuing education needs an Osler, a Dewey, or a Morrison. Both before and after one appears, however, it also needs a group of dedicated workers who look beyond the demands of the moment to catch a glimpse of what the institution might eventually become, and then devote their talents and their energies toward making that vision a reality.

BIBLIOGRAPHY

Alford, Harold J. Continuing Education in Action. New York: John Wiley and Sons, Inc., 1968.

Alford, Harold J. "A History of Residential Adult Education." Unpublished doctoral dissertation, The University of Chicago, 1966.

Bales, Robert F. "How People Interact in Conferences." Scientific American, Vol. CLXXXXII, 1955.

Beckhard, Richard. How to Plan and Conduct Workshops and Conferences. New York: Association Press, 1956.

Begtrup, Holger; Lund, Hans; and Manniche, Peter. The Folk High Schools of Denmark and the Development of a Farming Community. London: Oxford University Press, 1949.

Blakely, Robert. "How Does Short Term Learning Fulfill Societal Needs." NUEA Spectator, XXX (February-March, 1968).

Buskey, John H. "The Development and Testing of a Typology of Adult Education Programs in University Residential Centers." Unpublished doctoral dissertation, The University of Chicago, 1970.

Campbell, Olive Dame. The Danish Folk School. New York: Macmillan Company, 1928.

Capes, Mary, editor. Communication or Conflict. New York: Association Press, 1960.

Coleman, David S. "A Study of the Leader Behavior of Selected Directors of University Conference Operations." Unpublished doctoral dissertation, The University of Wisconsin, 1969.

Continuing Education Report. Numbers 5, 10. 11, 15, 16. The University of Chicago, 1965-1968.

Crane, Carlson E. "A Critical Analysis of Selected University Continuing Education Centers in the United States." Unpublished doctoral thesis, New York University, 1959.

Dekker, Tunis Henry. "Faculty Commitment to University Adult Education." Unpublished doctoral dissertation, The University of Chicago, 1965.

Deppe, Donald A. "The Adult Educator: Marginal Man and Boundary Definer," Adult Leadership, XVIII (October, 1969).

Deppe, Donald A. "The Conference Director as a Boundary Definer of the University." Unpublished doctoral dissertation, The University of Chicago, 1965.

Florell, Robert J. "Applicational Transfer in Adult Education." Unpublished doctoral dissertation, The University of Nebraska, 1966.

Fraser, W. R. Residential Education. Oxford: Pergamon Press, 1968.

Garside, Donald. "Short-Term Residential Colleges: Their Origins and Value." Studies in Adult Education, I (April, 1969).

Goodell, Frank C. "A Program Planning Checklist for the Meeting Planner." Adult Leadership, XVIII (December, 1969).

Hart, Joseph K. Light from the North: The Danish Folk High Schools and Their Meaning for America. New York: Henry Holt and Company, 1927.

Hennessy, Thomas C.S.J., editor. The Inner Crusade: The Closed Retreat in the United States. Chicago: Loyola University Press, 1965.

Hunter, Guy. Residential Colleges: Some New Developments in British Adult Education. Pasadena, California: Fund for Adult Education, n.d.

Jackson, Norman W. "An Exploratory Adult Education Program for Parents and Their Children of Senior High Age to Improve Communication in the Home." Unpublished doctoral dissertation, Indiana University, 1964.

Kafka, James J. "Determinants of Residential Adult Education Effectiveness." Unpublished doctoral dissertation, The University of Chicago, 1970.

Kindler, Herbert S. Organizing the Technical Conference. New York: Reinhold Publishing Corporation, 1960.

Lacognata, A.A. "A Comparison of the Effectiveness of Adult Residential and Non-Residential Learning Situations." Research Reports. Chicago: Center for the Study of Liberal Education for Adults, 1961.

Livingstone, Richard. "The Future in Education." On Education. New York: The Macmillan Company, 1964.

Loosely, Elizabeth. Residential Adult Education: A Canadian Voice. Canadian Association for Adult Education, 1960.

Lund, Ragnar, editor. Scandinavian Adult Education. Copenhagen: Det
   Danske Forlag, 1949.

Mead, Margaret and Byers, Paul. The Small Conference: An Innovation in
   Communication. Paris: Mouton and Co., 1968.

Mead, Margaret. "Conference Behavior." Columbia University Forum, X
   (Summer, 1967).

Miles, Matthew, "On Temporary Systems." Innovation in Education,
   Matthew Miles, editor. New York: Columbia University Press, 1966.

Miller, Paul. Excerpts from an Address. Occasional Papers, No. 1.
   New England Center for Continuing Education, October, 1966.

Newman, John Henry. University Sketches. Dublin: Browne and Nolan, Lt d.
   undated, text of 1856.

Pelton, Arthur E. "Financing Residential Adult and Continuing Education."
   Unpublished doctoral dissertation, The University of Nebraska, 1969.

Pitkin, Royce B. The Residential School in American Adult Education.
   Chicago: Center for the Study of Liberal Education for Adults, 1956.

Rogers, William C. "Wilton Park: International Conference Champion?"
   The NUEA Spectator, XXXIV (April-May, 1969).

Schacht, Robert H. "Residential Adult Education: An Analysis and Interpretation." Unpublished doctoral dissertation, The University of
   Wisconsin, 1957.

Schacht, Robert H. Week-End Learning in the U.S.A. Chicago: Center for
   the Study of Liberal Education for Adults, 1960.

Sheffield, Sherman. "The Orientations of Adult Continuing Learners." Unpublished doctoral dissertation, The University of Chicago, 1962.

Siegle, Peter E. "The International Conference on Residential Adult Education:
   An Interpretive Review." Adult Education, VI (Winter, 1956).

Smith, Robert M. "One Hundred and Fifty Institutes in Adult Education."
   Adult Leadership, XIV (September, 1965).

Speak, Lawrence. "Residential Adult Education in England." Unpublished
   master's thesis, Leeds University, 1969.

Stevenson, John H. "A Comparative Study of Residential and Non-Residential
   Adult Religious Education Programs." Unpublished doctoral thesis,
   Indiana University, 1968.

Stock, Arthur. "A Time to Confer?" Adult Education, British, XLI (September, 1968).

Sulkin, Howard. "Relationship between Participant Personality and Teaching Methods in Management Training." Unpublished doctoral dissertation, The University of Chicago, 1969.

Thelen, Herbert. Role Perception and Task Performance of Experimentally Composed Small Groups. Report #1 from N.I.M.H. Project " Use of Small Groups to Adapt Problem Students, " 1965-1970.

Thomas, George B. "Learning at a Conference." Phi Delta Kappan (April, 1968).

Waller, Ross D. Methods at Holly Royde. London: National Institute of Adult Education, 1965.

Welden, J. Eugene. "Program Planning and Program Effectiveness in University Residential Centers." Unpublished doctoral dissertation, The University of Chicago, 1966.

White, Thurman. "Financing Residential Centers for Continuing Education," NUEA Spectator, April-May, 1971.

Zelko, Harry P. The Business Conference. New York: McGraw-Hill Book Company, 1969.

Other recent Notes and Essays of the Syracuse University Publications in Continuing Education include:

69. ENDS AND MEANS: THE NATIONAL CONFERENCE ON CONTIN-
UING EDUCATION IN NURSING, 1970, ed. by Ruth McHenry. Papers
cover subjects such as resources, principles of organization, and
strategies for change. Among the authors included are George Beal and
Joe M. Bohlen, Betty Gwaltney, Dr. Charles H. Russell, Dr. Mary
Dineen, Dr. H. Peplau, Clifford L. Winters, Jr. May 1971 115 p $ 2.50

68. SENSITIVITY TRAINING: PROCESSES, PROBLEMS, AND APPLI-
CATIONS, by Arthur Blumberg. In Dr. Blumberg's words, "the attempt
throughout the monograph is to clarify the nature of sensitivity training
and let the reader draw his own conclusions about its efficacy and appro-
priateness in any particular situation." April 1971. 90 p $2.50

67. TOWARD THE EDUCATIVE SOCIETY, Project Director: Alexander
N. Charters. Essays that study ways by which elementary and secondary
schools in the U.S. could better enable young people to become life-long
learners. January 1971 94 p $ 2.50

66. ESSAYS ON THE FUTURE OF CONTINUING EDUCATION WORLD-
WIDE, ed. by Warren Ziegler. Papers presented at an International
Seminar on Adult Education held at Syracuse University in December,
1969. July 1970 141 p $ 3.00

65. ESSAYS ON NEW CAREERS: SOCIAL IMPLICATIONS FOR ADULTS
EDUCATORS, by Frank Riessman, Alan Gartner, Sumner Rosen, and
Joseph Featherstone. Essays that deal with some of the most fundamental
challenges to adult educators and the establishment they represent.
June 1970 81 p $ 2.50

64. THE UNIVERSITY AND COMMUNITY SERVICE: PERSPECTIVES
FOR THE SEVENTIES, ed. by James B. Whipple and Doris S. Chertow.
Five papers written by members of the University Council on Education
for Public Responsibility. May 1970 85 p $ 2.50

63. KNOWLEDGE IS POWER TO CONTROL POWER: NEW INSTITUTIONAL
ARRANGEMENTS AND ORGANIZATIONAL PATTERNS FOR CONTIN-
UING EDUCATION, R.J. Blakely and Ivan M. Lappin. A study con-
ducted for the U.S. Office of Education in 1969. 1969 88 p $ 2.50

62. DILEMMAS OF AMERICAN POLICY: CRUCIAL ISSUES IN CONTEM-
PORARY SOCIETY, Samuel DuBois Cook, George G. Stern, Thomas F.
Green, Anthony S. Weiner. Papers on the Negro Revolution, the generation gap, post-secondary education, and war and American society.
1969 108 p $ 3.00

Order from:

SYRACUSE UNIVERSITY PRESS
Box 8, University Station
Syracuse, New York 13210